Apostle Walter E. Roberts

**Presiding Bishop and Chief Apostle,
HEAL THE NATIONS:
Global Fellowship of Ministries**

I LIVE TO PRAY

DEDICATION

My Father, Pastor and Assistant District Superintendant James Thomas Roberts, Sr.; My Mother, District Missionary Gloria Renida Dix Roberts; Apostle Ernest Joseph Mathews, Jr; (Bishop),Superintendant Leo Hughey, Jr; Mother Idella Sawyer; Bishop Otis Lockett Sr.; Mother Eugenia Rorie, Mother Carie Young, Apostle-Archbishop Milton F. Perry; Bishop John L. Hines; Mother DeLois Zachery; Bishop William Isaac Powell, Apostle Essie Powell; Apostolic Prophet, Bishop Elect William Ellis; Mrs. Gordon, "Mom" Freda Lindsay; Superintendant Nebo and Mother Mattie Roberts; Pastor Oliver Agee; Mother Handy, Mother Russ, Mother Katie B. Haines, Mother Eliza Williams, Deacon Thomas Waye; Deacon Walter Kent; Elder James Smith, Mother Smith, Bishop LeRoy Anderson; Administrative Assistant Superintendant Hyrd Seals; Mother Marva Fears, Mother Mary Lane............. Each of these people left an indelible mark on my life that can never be erased. They have gone on before me and transitioned, by HIS grace, into "The Rest" of The LORD. They prayed for me, mentored me, and spoke prophetically over me, and I live through their prayers and their words, as well as the prayers and words that have been and continue to be spoken over my life, by those of you who are alive and remain. I LOVE U all, and I give special recognition to two Anointed and Loving Women of GOD Mother Beatrice Matthews Church Mother and Widow of the Founder of Greater Evangelical COGIC, and COGIC WNY Jurisdiction #2 State Supervisor of Women Mother Wilma J. Hughey. Great Grace, to both of you.

Finally, I must acknowledge, that I would not be who I am, without the years of support and strength of loving relationship of Pastor Regenia Roberts and my children and grandchildren, Elder Walter E. Roberts, II, Charnica, Jadyn, and Walter E. Roberts, III(King). Elder Phoebe Marie Roberts, and Elder James T. Roberts, III. Thank you I am honored to love you.

Acknowledgements

John Donne said, "No man is an island, entire of itself..."

That is the truth which embodies my existence, so It is just a right thing to acknowledge each of the following people: every partner of Our Lord's Temple COGIC, Refuge Center Ministries, Mt. Nebo GCOG, Covenant Community Fellowship Church, and Covenant Life COGIC who served and partnered with me in those ministries as the Pastor and Bishop, My Apostolic Administrative Staff, Associates, Sons, Daughters, and Covering; without whose contributions, prayers, and encouragement this book would still be just a thought.

My Spiritual Sons and Daughters Apostle O. Deshea and Pastor Jacqueline Cuthrell, Ministers Jody, Hannah, and my Granddaughter Reese Catherine Edmonds; Apostles Anthony and Maxine Hairston; My Apostolic Advisory Staff Elder Walter E. Roberts, II, Mrs. Charnica Roberts

Marketing Consultants, Elder James T. Roberts, III media and technology, Elder Phoebe Roberts-Lewis Support, Minister C.T. Frances graphic design and web creation, Prophet J. Valencia Cross administration and promotions, and Elder Cathy Black Apostolic Secretary; My Apostolic Board and Covering: Apostle Monroe Hodges, Apostle Shirley Wade-Anthony, Apostolic Prophet Beth Nicholls, Apostle Robert Crisman; Prayer Partners and Encouragers: Apostle Harold L. Harris, Bishop James C. and Lady Joyce Hash, Lady Barbara T. Lockett, Bishop John C. and Lady Janice McClurkin, Bishop Ralph and Lady Dianne Lewis, Minister Rose M. Shuman, Psalmist Lynn Pearce, Brother Horatio Denson, Elder John Brincefield, Apostle James and Lady Gwenderlyn Ramsey, Bishop Stephanie Stratford, Apostle David and Pastor Lori Stroman, Deacon Tommy Fears, Prophet Debra Faulkner; Apostle Tommy and Pastor Lynette Roberts. With these people in my life and through the grace of GOD, I have traveled from a place of eternal transition, to the renewal of strength and purpose. In spite of the prognosis of death from Physicians, and through 17 surgeries GOD has used these people to enlarge my life in the earth. Thank you all. The best is yet to come.

Special Thanks to Evangelist Missionary Patrisha Blue for her assistance with obtaining Historical Information included in this book. Thank you for strengthening my thought process on the completion of this book.

"Well Church"

Well Church,

I don come out here this evening,

For to tell you my desire.

I don said I would not tell it,

But my soul's been caught on fire.

Every since that Sunday evening,

Down at that little shack,

I don gave my heart to Jesus,

And I never shall go back....

This Poem was written by Mother Idella Sawyer. She served as the Church Mother to my Father Pastor James T. Roberts, Sr. Also she was so encouraging and strengthening as the Church Mother during my time as Pastor as well. After that time she served her son Pastor Csiko Sawyer at Oasis Fellowship in Ithaca, NY. She was a Prayer Warrior and an Intercessor.

Table of Contents:

Dedication

Acknowledgements

"Well Church"

Table of Contents

Part 1: My Pursuit of HIS Presence

Testimony

Notes

Why I Pray

What is Prayer?

Constrained to Pray

Lingering Questions

Part 2: It's Time to Pray

1. All Kinds of Prayer

2. Prayer of Petition

3. Prayer of Thanksgiving

4. Prayer of Agreement

5. Prayer of Repentance

6. Worship and Praise the Sound of Prayer

7. Praying the Word of GOD

8. Praying In Tongues

9. Intercession

10. Travailing to Prevailing

11. Warfare Prayer

12. Prayer and Fasting

13. Prayers That I Pray Daily

Closing Thoughts

Scriptural Reference Index

Contact Information

IMPART LA Church Logo

HEAL THE NATIONS Logo

Testimony

September 21, 2015

I am beginning this book under the Unction of HOLY SPIRIT. I have just ended a session of prayer in which I was constrained to begin and trust that HOLY SPIRIT will guide me to the completion of this endeavor. What I am doing now should largely be considered background notes for me to remember and possibly share with a few people close to me at a later date. I confess that I have no set date of completion for this book. It is my goal as I begin this work, to spend time everyday moving forward toward its completion. I am thanking The FATHER in advance, for all of the people in my life who are praying for me. I know that there are those that pray daily, and those that pray frequently, and some who pray occasionally, but whenever they lift my name into the spirit realm, I am thankful for them. I don't know if they realize how powerful their prayers are, but I am thankful, because I believe that it is those prayers, even those that were offered on my behalf by some Men and Women of God who have transitioned into their rest in the presence of The Lord, that have kept me to this point in my life, and will continue to take me to the completion of my assignment within the Plan of GOD for my life.

Just as a point of reference, I am currently residing in the city of Arlington Texas. Arlington is the third largest municipality within the Dallas/Fortworth Metroplex. I have been residing in the Metroplex for 1 year and 47 days now. I do not have the energy to put into words the complete history of my experiences over that period of time. Those of you who are close to me in my life, already know some if not all of the events which have led to me relocating from Winston Salem, North Carolina to this exciting, fast paced, rapidly growing region of the country. Suffice it to say that I have embraced with Thanksgiving; The FATHER's leading me to this region. Where my life goes from here is not due to any personal agenda of my own, neither to any personal vision, especially since I never envisioned this reality in my life. So, "I Live To Pray" is birthed out of what I have come to identify as the "Unusual Reality" of my existence in the earth. Up to this point I have shed many tears and battled personal mental degradation, and won the fight over the spirit of depression to survive and arrive at this New Beginning.

About a month ago, I was hard at work in a Williamson Dickeys warehouse in North Fort Worth, doing my best to have a steady income and make sure that my bills were paid. I wanted to ensure that I would not have to make any more desperate pleas for help from the people who love me most in ministry. However, that job as had happened with each of the three proceeding jobs that I had been blessed to obtain since my arrival, came to a screeching halt. This time the cause was a spirit of affliction which I have been winning the battle over for the last 18 years of my life. So as I write these words this morning, I am dealing with the effects of this disease, but I am strengthened by the voice of HOLY SPIRIT that the time of complete wholeness for me is at hand. So a few days after this last flare up, I received a call from one of my dearest friends in the world. She has been a faithful supporter of my Ministry and Family for more than 20 years. Prophetess Rose Shuman called to check on me one evening and to encourage me. She asked me at that time, if I would send her some of my manuscripts that I had previously written so that her new publishing company within Elijah's Herald could publish it for me. Sadly, I had to share with her the unfortunate circumstances by which my previous manuscripts had been lost. However in that same moment I felt a new desire to begin again. I also felt that after all that I have been through and what was yet to come, anything that HOLY SPIRIT empowered me to write in this season of my life, would undoubtedly be more relevant and more effective for practical ministry, than anything I could possibly have written before. It is certain that I no longer view ministry from the same perspective. My life has changed. The things that I have personally experienced in the last 5 years have so dramatically altered my perspective of my walk with GOD. That person I used to be would be barely recognizable by the people who have and will encounter me going forward.

Another moment of revelation came a couple of weeks ago, when my friend and brother Apostle James Ramsey called to check on my well being. It was during that conversation that I heard the voice of HOLY SPIRIT compel me to say to James, "I Live to Pray. That's what I do, that's what I was created for. That's what HOLY SPIRIT was telling me over 6 years ago, during one of my 40 day times of consecration. I live to Pray. I am going to write that book."

However, I have been battling my physical condition in order to find the strength to begin this endeavor. Today marks the beginning of what I trust by HOLY SPIRIT, will be a literary work of HOLY SPIRIT expressed through my life and HIS WORD. I ask and trust HIM for HIS guidance and direction, as HE gives LIFE and POWER to what is written within the pages of this book, so that the letter will not be able to kill what HOLY SPIRIT has given Life to.

Walter Earl Roberts…….. I Live To Pray.

When I wrote those words, I thought at that time, that I would surely begin to write continually from there, and this book would have been completed by now. After that time in late 2015, I became floor bound for most of 2016 due to the deterioration of my health. Thank you to my younger brother, Apostle Tommy Roberts and My youngest Son Elder James T. Roberts, III. They worked together to relocate me from Arlington Texas, to Tiffin, Iowa. It was at the point of death that GOD used them along with my wonderful Sister in love Pastor Lynette Roberts, and the wonderful family of Lifepointe Christian Faith Center to support and strengthen me through the next two full years of medical treatment, surgeries, and recovery.

Also, I would like to thank GOD for the medical staff of the University of Iowa Hospitals and Clinics, in Iowa City, Iowa. Thank you for allowing GOD to use you to treat me, even though you told me from the beginning, that the issues in my body were incurable. I will forever be grateful for the consistent kindness, compassion, excellence, and professionalism shown to me during that time. At each subsequent visit, I have continued to receive the same wonderful care and attention.

There are other ministry associates and loved ones who I have not taken the time to mention in either the dedication or this portion of my Testimony, but they have been instrumental in getting me to this point. I love you all.

NOTES

What are you in the process of becoming? I pray that everyone who reads this book will begin a new journey in their own Personal Passionate Pursuit of HIS Presence.

More:

A Personal, Passionate, Pursuit of HIS Presence; will make you Purposeful, Powerful, and Productive***** Me

Prayer is not an Accidental Activity; It must be Intentional……….4am 10/9/15

Notes:

Philippians 3.10

"That I may know him, and the power of his resurrection, and the fellowship of his sufferings, being made conformable unto his death;"
Philippians 3:10 KJV

"[For my determined purpose is] that I may know Him [that I may progressively become more deeply and intimately acquainted with Him, perceiving and recognizing and understanding the wonders of His Person more strongly and more clearly], and that I may in that same way come to know the power outflowing from His resurrection [which it exerts over believers], and that I may so share His sufferings as to be continually transformed [in spirit into His likeness even] to His death, [in the hope]"
Philippians 3:10 AMPC

"I gave up all that inferior stuff so I could know Christ personally, experience his resurrection power, be a partner in his suffering, and go all the way with him to death itself. If there was any way to get in on the resurrection from the dead, I wanted to do it."
Philippians 3:10-11 MSG

I have been driven and guided my whole spiritual life by this verse of scripture. It has been the one constant, no matter what place or stage of life I have found myself in. "That I may know HIM…," the HIM from whom I derive my essential purpose in life. It is HIM who has been the focal point of everything else; no matter what I am it is due to my pursuit of wanting to know HIM. From this point of reference, I hold myself accountable even through bad decisions and difficult circumstances.

For in him we live, and move, and have our being; as certain also of your own poets have said, For we are also his offspring.
Acts 17:28 KJV

"It is through him that we live and function and have our identity; just as your own poets have said, 'Our lineage comes from him.'" Acts 17:28 TPT

'By his power we live and move and exist.' Some of your own poets have said: 'For we are his children.'
Acts 17:28 NCV

My life is no longer my own. I live in union and in fellowship with HIM. When JESUS became CHRIST in my life, I freely and joyfully surrendered control to HIM. I live to fulfill HIS purpose and complete the Kingdom activities which HE has assigned to me. I live in HIM, and exist to expand HIS Kingdom in the earth. HE also lets me enjoy the life HE gave me to live. And living in fellowship with HIM is a win- win for both of us, and the world.

It is this unshakeable desire that centers me. Halleluiah! I live to Pray, because it is through this spiritual dialogue called prayer, that I am able to fellowship with HIM.

Prayer in its truest form must be a dialogue and not a monologue of our wants needs and personal issues. Never think that HE is not listening, but I would rather spend 5 seconds listening for the opportunity to hear from HIM, than to boast of 5 hours that were spent with HIM listening to me. HE knows me better than I know myself; therefore HE doesn't need to hear me as much as I need to hear HIM. I have long believed that the scriptures which encourage us to come to HIM, to bring our petitions to HIM, are just a way for HOLY SPIRIT to get us into that place of presence. Once there, if our hearts are truly open to HIM we become overwhelmed by the sheer magnitude of HIS presence. So much so, that the awesome revelation of who HE is should quickly overshadow our selfish motives for praying in the first place. HE is always aware of my needs. If as a student of the word, I believe this, then it must follow, that HE has also provided for those needs before I even ask.

"Wherefore, if God so clothe the grass of the field, which to day is, and to morrow is cast into the oven, shall he not much more clothe you, O ye of little faith? Therefore take no thought, saying, What shall we eat? or, What shall we drink? or, Wherewithal shall we be clothed? (For after all these things do the Gentiles seek:) for your heavenly Father knoweth that ye have need of all these things. But seek ye first the kingdom of God, and his righteousness; and all these things shall be added unto you."
Matthew 6:30-33 KJV

"But if God so clothes the grass of the field, which today is alive and green and tomorrow is tossed into the furnace, will He not much more surely clothe you, O you of little faith? Therefore do not worry and be anxious, saying, What are we going to have to eat? or, What are we going to have to drink? or, What are we going to have to wear? For the Gentiles (heathen) wish for and crave and diligently seek all these things, and your heavenly Father knows well that you need them all. But seek (aim at and strive after) first of all His kingdom and His righteousness (His way of doing and being right), and then all these things taken together will be given you besides."
Matthew 6:30-33 AMPC

A few years ago I read this scripture and HOLY SPIRIT quickened verse 32 within me. GOD knows what things I have need of. After that revelation, I decided that it seems redundant to pray about my needs. Understand, I am not telling you not to pray about your needs. I just have a peace that my Heavenly Father is going to supply all of my needs. (Philippians 4.19) So, therefore it is more profitable for me to spend time in prayer searching for, and longing for revelations of HIS reality, that have not already been revealed to me, and maybe not to any man…….

"Call unto me, and I will answer thee, and shew thee great and mighty things, which thou knowest not."
Jeremiah 33:3 KJV

"Call to Me and I will answer you and show you great and mighty things, fenced in and hidden, which you do not know (do not distinguish and recognize, have knowledge of and understand)."
Jeremiah 33:3 AMPC

'Judah, pray to me, and I will answer you. I will tell you important secrets you have never heard before.'
Jeremiah 33:3 NCV

I call that fellowship with The Father. It is purposeful fellowship which allows me to spend intimate time with HIM, getting to know HIM.

"Just like Sweet Honey in the Rock, Oh just like sweet honey in the rock. Oh taste and see that the LORD is Good, Just like sweet honey in the rock"

These are the words of the song that I would hear several times a week at 12 noon sharp as my Mother, my Brother Tommy, and I would participate at the home of two of the most precious Sisters the Kingdom of God ever produced, Mother Williams and Mother Haines in Geneva, New York. My precious Mother would gather up my brother and I; when the weather was good I would get to ride my tricycle, and she would hustle us down the street several blocks from our house at 16 Middle Street in Geneva, New York, to the home of Mother Eliza Williams and Mother Katie B. Haines. These two Church Mothers of Mt. Calvary COGIC would have daily prayer in their home at 12noon sharp. They started on time, but I figure that due to the fact that my Mother was dealing with a two year old and a three year old, it was probably something that she had to do for us, which made us occasionally late arriving. However, the door would always be unlocked, and we would go right in. Inevitably, the Mothers would have already started their daily prayer time. On rare occasions I can remember that there were one or two others who attended the prayer meetings. However, my greatest memories are of that song, and of the ferverency with which these women sought the presence of The LORD. Later in my life during my early teen age years, My Father began the task of planting a new ministry in Ithaca,

New York. Sometime in 1973, Gethsemane COGIC was born. My Parents, and the last three of us who were still forced to accompany my parents, would travel from Romulus, NY, to Geneva, NY on Friday nights. There we would pick up Mother Haines and Mother Williams who worked in the early days to help my Father and Mother as they labored to plant a new ministry in Ithaca, NY. To this day, I remain amazed by the magnitude of their commitment to the ministry of the gospel. As I think back upon what it took for my father and mother to work full time jobs which required them to drive 45 miles to work one way and then drive back after work; come home get cleaned up and dressed, often without eating dinner, drive 30 miles to pick up these two Women of GOD, and then travel back the other direction another 60 miles total to Ithaca, New York. We would arrive at a place of ministry in an elderly Seventh Day Adventist Mother's home. I still don't know how GOD was able to touch her heart, except that I know GOD gave my Parents favor through the woman who served as Gethsemane COGIC's Church Mother for several years, Mother Mozelle Kinsey. We would arrive there and immediately begin praying. Not just an invocation, but a ferverent effort to open heaven over that little home on the Southside of Ithaca, NY. Then often because my father tended to be exuberantly vociferous in is preaching, we would dismiss service, usually after 11pm, and head back toward Geneva, NY to drop off Mother Williams and Mother Haines, before heading to our home in Romulus, NY. (Often on those Friday nights we would be blessed by Elder Ernest and Mother Beatrice Matthews, Deacon Thomas Waye, Elder Oliver Agee, and Mother Mary Lane.)

These are the types of events and experiences which impacted my life and helped shape my current paradigm concerning pursuing the presence of GOD in prayer, even without me realizing it.

11/3/15

2:27amcst

As I kneel beside my bed, the sounds of a song sung by Patrick Dopson, entitled "Keep Me", are playing in this time of Personal Pursuit of HIS Presence. When I use the terminology which HOLY SPIRIT gave me in 2010: Purposeful, Powerful, Personal and Passionate Pursuit, of HIS Presence, I do not wish to imply that it is a difficult thing to find HIM, or to enter into HIS presence. I remember during that time of fellowship, HE spoke to me and told me, "Walter I don't want you to make pursing ME sound like a difficult activity. I am not hiding from you. Did not I tell you, 'If you would draw near to ME, that I would draw near to you?' I long for your presence, even as you long for MINE."

It is my time of prayer, my moments of entering into HIS Presence. I long so much for the opportunity to lose myself IN HIM.

In these moments tonight, I am struggling in my flesh, to overcome an extreme sense of loneliness, and emptiness in my life. As I continue the process of healing in my body, I am unable to work in a secular job, something which I have never been reluctant to do. Not because I am afraid to, but in this moment, I am without the physical ability to do so. So, as I long for the manifestation of a plan or a clear path in which to walk, I am mentally drained by my uncharted course each day in this season.

It is that uncharted course, here in this moment; that sense of the unknown plans that HE has for me, which requires me to trust HIM completely. In order to do so successfully, I have to find a way to overwhelm the enemy's desire to trap me in fear. This is a battle I have already won, but I have come to realize that when I get to this place where I feel emptier than I do full, that I must seek HIS Presence. I must seek that place of covering.

"He that dwelleth in the secret place of the most High shall abide under the shadow of the Almighty."
Psalms 91:1 KJV

"Those who go to God Most High for safety will be protected by the Almighty."
Psalms 91:1 NCV

  I have come to depend upon these times so much. I have discovered that my time of Fellowship with The

FATHER is my most powerful contribution to the success of everyone connected to me, whether by blood or covenant. I understand fully my assignment in the earth. I Live to Pray. I get the opportunity to lay prostrate before HIM, and use my mouth to come into agreement with the heart of GOD. Out of my heart flows the words which, spoken by my tongue and lips, give HOLY SPIRIT the raw materials of creation for the will of GOD in the earth. HE speaks through me, the Angels hear and obey, and things happen. Miracles come forth; the will of GOD comes into being in the earth. Thy Kingdom come, Thy will be done...Psalms 103.20.

"Bless the Lord , ye his angels, that excel in strength, that do his commandments, hearkening unto the voice of his word."
Psalms 103:20 KJV

I pray because I need HIS presence. I pray and I worship HIM. In HIS presence is fullness of Joy. I pray because I need HIM to change me more than I need HIM to change anyone else. It is my greatest desire that I will become enough like HIM that people who meet me will be so impacted, that they will inquire as to what it is about me that is different from anyone else they know. In so doing I will be able to point them to HIM. I don't use my prayer time to try to affect anyone else's life. I do pray for the needs that people request me to pray for. But I never use my prayer time to deal with any personal issues that I am having with anyone in my life. People are not my enemy. I don't wrestle with flesh and blood... *Ephesians 6.10* Change me HOLY SPIRIT. Speak to me. Reveal to me Your Plan for me. What is Your Command for me? Show me Your assignment for me. I truly believe that my obedience to the revealed and assigned will of GOD for me, in conjunction with the obedience of others, to the assigned will of GOD for them, is more powerful than my asking GOD to change the minds of a congressman and judge. My obedience will bring the desired effect designed by the mind of GOD. Change me so that I become more sensitive, and cooperative with YOUR plans. Speak to me HOLY SPIRIT, that I may know YOUR plan for today as I receive confirmation of the Holy Word written in my heart,

I have to be here. I have to be here in YOUR presence FATHER. I have no strength of my own. I have no plans of my own. Everything that I have previously tried to do on my own has failed. I need YOU to define my purpose. In YOU I Live, In YOU I Move, In YOU I have my Being. I am thankful for the revelation that YOU share with me, but I am more appreciative of the privilege of being received into YOUR Presence. I hear YOU saying, "If all of MY children knew what a great privilege I had given them, to come boldly into MY Presence, to draw near with a pure heart in full assurance of faith; if they truly knew that Their FATHER would never turn them away, they would run through any struggle just to get here. Walter, do you know why the enemy fights you so hard in your prayer life, why he does everything he can to rob you of the time you spend with ME? It's because he knows that the more time you spend with ME, the more of ME gets inside you, and you become more than he can handle in the earth. If you are full of ME, then none of his deceptions work against you, and he has to try deceiving those around you in order to get you distracted and out of position. Do you realize how valuable the position in MY Presence is that you occupy? You must do all that you can to overcome every obstacle to maintain this place in MY Presence. It is not a singular place, as if to imply that it is any more special than the place I desire for all of MY children to occupy, but it is your place with ME. It is the place that I have reserved for you. It is the place where MY ear is inclined to the sound of your voice. It is the place where revelation is shared with you. It is the place where instructions are given to you concerning your assignment in MY plan. It is the place where Angelic hosts are summoned and dispatched according to what they hear ME saying through you. This place is your place. Never let it go, never allow anything to keep you from this place. In this place you are already made whole, so that you may go back to your assignment in the earth and share that wholeness with everyone you meet. It happens in this place."

I wonder how many Christians really understand who their real enemy is. For if they are not truly aware of the real enemy or his tactics, then they will be altogether inadequate in the daily struggles to possess and maintain, the victory which CHRIST JESUS our Savior has already won for us.

So too, if we are not aware of the real enemy, then we will be ignorant and ineffective in our efforts to defeat him in our personal struggles.

Enter In, Enter In

All we really need to do is to enter in to the presence of GOD. HE awaits the arrival of HIS children. The place of prayer is such a powerful place. (The place where Prayer was *WANT* to be made)

"And on the sabbath we went out of the city by a river side, where prayer was wont to be made; and we sat down, and spake unto the women which resorted thither."
Acts 16:13 KJV

"On the Sabbath, we left the city and went down along the river where we had heard there was to be a prayer meeting. We took our place with the women who had gathered there and talked with them. One woman, Lydia, was from Thyatira and a dealer in expensive textiles, known to be a God-fearing woman. As she listened with intensity to what was being said, the Master gave her a trusting heart—and she believed!"
Acts 16:13-14 MSG

"And on the Sabbath day we went outside the [city's] gate to the bank of the river where we supposed there was an [accustomed] place of prayer, and we sat down and addressed the women who had assembled there."
Acts 16:13 AMPC

"On the day of worship we went out of the city to a place along the river where we thought Jewish people gathered for prayer. We sat down and began talking to the women who had gathered there."
Acts 16:13 GW

"On the Sabbath day we went outside the city gate to the river where we thought we would find a special place for prayer. Some women had gathered there, so we sat down and talked with them."
Acts 16:13 NCV

Not speaking of Place, as in a geographic location, but rather as a spiritual realm. It can be wherever we are physically, but once we commit ourselves to prayer in that time and enter in, we are elevated into a spiritual realm and coming into agreement and fellowship with HE who defines our Purpose and gives us our assignment in the earth.

There is also significance to the Time of Prayer. There is significance to the place of prayer, and the time of prayer. Because The Kingdom of Heaven and The Kingdom of GOD exist in Eternity, every Moment is an Eternal Moment. Therefore, when we enter in to the Presence of The FATHER, that time of prayer becomes an eternal time. So what we accomplish during those Moments effects Eternity on a level that extends far beyond our natural understanding.

HOLY SPIRIT said to me, that in the moments that Sons and Daughters give themselves over to HIS will in prayer, demonic destruction is averted; the plans and plots of darkness are disrupted and literally exposed, uprooted, and destroyed. Our prayer in The SPIRIT assists and empowers Angelic activity that very few believers understand is even possible. This is why the enemy works so hard to stop us from praying. HOLY SPIRIT also said to me. That often many lives are saved and delivered from destruction because we have implemented eternal changes in the Spirit realm through our obedience in prayer. Oh how powerful we become to Heaven when we pray. Preaching releases Faith for Salvation, but Prayer empowers the Plan of Salvation to continue to operate effectively in the earth. Prayer is the Spiritual nourishment which feeds and strengthens the foundational purpose of GOD which initiated and created the Church and supports its HOLY SPIRIT authorized activities; "…Thy will be done, on earth as it is in Heaven."

Sunday December 20, 2015

I don't really know how to classify this entry. I have been battling such a severe physical attack over the last 4 plus months that I have barely been able to get out of the bed, much less get out of the apartment. However, on Thursday December 17, 2015, as I was praying, I felt strong enough to put my sweat suit on, and go outside to do a prayer walk. Quite honestly, I hadn't done a prayer walk since 2010. I was doing regular prayer walks during that time, until I developed a stress fracture in my foot and was forced to stop. Thursday morning I walked around the complex and it took approximately 30 minutes to circle the property. I had been praying for about 30 minutes before I started the walk, and when I came back into my apartment, I prayed another hour before I began to lose focus. Approximately 30 minutes after completing my structured prayer time, I received a text message from an apostolic brother of mine whom I hadn't communicated with for many months, and I haven't really discussed Ministry with him in years. He began to tell me some things prophetically concerning my future in Ministry and I received it. We ended our communication after about 30 minutes. As I was preparing to lie down to rest, My Brother, from Iowa who is also an Apostle and a Pastor, sent me a text message to ask when we could talk. I told him that the best time was immediately, as I would soon be asleep. As we spoke, He began to share with me some of the exact things concerning my life and Ministry that the other Apostle had shared with me. This was very exciting for me. I included this information to reveal that the last two days since this experience have been extremely tiring and physically challenging for me.

However, this morning, Sunday December 20, 2015 I was strengthened again by HOLY SPIRIT to resume prayer walking. As I was beginning the walk this morning, I was impressed by HOLY SPIRIT to remember, that my most successful time in Pastoral Ministry, came as a direct result of Prayer Walks. I can't really tell you why this has not been a constant part of my existence all of these years. I can tell you, that life has a way of distracting us from our purpose in the plan of GOD. I am confident that the reason for my including this experience in the pages of this book is because HOLY SPIRIT has informed me that

I am not the only man or woman called by GOD, who has been challenged by the spirit of distraction. It is so easy to get caught up in the subtle infiltrations of the enemy into our lives, that it gives me a fresh revelation on, Ecclesiastes………. "it is the little foxes that destroy the vine." Often I have discovered that the framework of my life, my marriage, my health, my finances, and my ministry have been destroyed because the little foxes were able to infiltrate into areas that I had begun to take for granted. As I write these things this morning, I am persuaded that the only way to overcome the illegitimate infiltration, or said another way, the trespasses of demonic spirits into our lives, is to remain vigilant in our fellowship in the presence of The FATHER. Only by maintaining an open communication through HOLY SPIRIT, can we remain sharpened and focused in our ability to discern the enemy's attempts to distract us and get us off course and off purpose and assignment. I am expecting to receive new and exciting encounters with HOLY SPIRIT, as I continue to gain strength and resume these prayer walks. Remember, I Live To Pray!

June 20, 2016

If MY people whom I have called to Pray only knew the impact of their words within the spirit realm, they would never hesitate when I call them to spend time opening their mouths and releasing their voice before My Presence. Oh what miracles and victorious living they would experience.
(Personal fellowship with The Father)

WHY I PRAY

I remember those days very clearly. There is a particular day, in 1964. It's amazing to sit here reliving this moment……. My Mother, Gloria, is walking briskly down the street in Geneva, NY. She is carrying my younger brother Tommy and encouraging me to keep up as she moves swiftly down the street. I don't know why she allowed me to ride my tricycle that day, because it didn't always happen. But, she was such a wonderfully loving woman, that she may have just been indulging my desire, in an effort to get there without having to struggle with a three year old with an attitude, and potentially adding to an already challenging situation while carrying a two year old.

While I clearly remember those moments, they exist within a larger more powerful and impactful memory. Fore, a few minutes later, my mother was exhorting me to come quietly through the back door of the house and enter into this place which clearly was different from the house we lived in. The greatest difference I remember was the almost total quietness, (Our house was almost never quiet. That was because there were 8 children and 2 parents present for a great majority of the time.) But as we turned a slight corner through the kitchen my mother pushed aside a curtain which covered a doorway, seemingly the curtain took the place of a solid door, and provided a semblance of privacy for the activities within the room. As we entered the room, there were two women present in the room. I remember thinking how interesting it was that they showed no alarm and were not the least bit disturbed by our arrival. They were singing…….. My mother ushered me to a chair and placed my bother Tommy down as well, and began to sing along with the two older women (I have to stop and tell you of how difficult it is to get through this memory. I am paralyzed by the fact that there is such a genuinely powerful presence in this memory. How incapable I am to prevent the tears from rolling down my face in this moment, as I sit at this computer experiencing a tangible presence of GOD. How it challenges me, and arrests me as I realize, that the power of the presence which I was entering into in that room, is able to minister to me now, and inspire me to lift my hands in worship even now 54 years later. Hallelujah!!!)

Those two precious and powerful "Mothers of Zion," as the church used to call them were clearly caught up in the realm of worship, inspired by HOLY SPIRIT's presence there in that little room, Mother Haines, and Mother Williams were singing and giving praise to GOD. How wonderful it is to still have the memory of their voices. With Mother Haines playing the tambourine as they sung,

"Just like sweet honey in the rock; Ohhh just like sweet honey in the rock. Oh taste and see, that the Lord is good. Just like sweet honey in the rock."

Through their song, they were able to demonstrate that certain, "sound of prayer." I was sharing with a close friend, who is also a powerfully anointed intercessor. She mentioned to me, that when she goes before the LORD in a corporate setting, one of the things that bless her is the certain, "sound of prayer." There is an audible crying out to GOD and the crying out to the FATHER is representative of our heart's desire to make a true connection with the presence of GOD. That song, and that sound; oh how wonderful.

As I sat there on that sofa, a three year old boy, I was captivated by that song. I have remembered it throughout my entire life. I can even remember my mother singing it at various times as I grew older. I wasn't caught up in the prayer time which followed the singing. But rather, it was the words which were stuck in my mind. "….. Oh taste and see, that the Lord is good…." I would often wonder how they had discovered so certainly, that the Lord was/is good. Since those days, I have lived with a consuming motivation to know, that LORD who is good.

I don't know if I have a theological answer to give people who inquire concerning My Prayer life. What I am able to tell them, is that there is a hunger and a thirst for the presence of GOD, which consumes me. No matter how much I pray, I always want to pray some more. But if there is any one experience which exists as a catalyst for my desire and love of prayer, it is the question of; why those Mothers were so certain, that the Lord is good?

Let me tell you a little about myself, I am a child of "The Church." I was born in Geneva, NY to a mother who was a born again Christian, and a father who would soon give his life to CHRIST sometime within a year of my birth. Maybe I will get the chance to write about his extraordinary conversion experience at another time. But through their personal conversion to becoming a disciple of JESUS the CHRIST, I became a defacto church member. I grew up in the church. I spent days and nights in the church. Many Sundays, we would have three services, which required us to eat our meals at the church as well. There was even one time when I was four years old, that I woke up from being asleep on the church pew. Seeing that the building was empty, I left the building and walked home. It wasn't such a big deal, since we lived down the block from the church at the time. When I walked into the kitchen of the house, I asked my mother why they left me in the church, she said, "We weren't worried. You knew your way home." (Oh how times have changed. Also, that's the only time that I can remember my mother having jokes.) I believe that we as humans are on a course that allows us to align with the Plan of GOD, and set in motion our true reason for existing. Let me explain this thought. After starting Kindergarten in Geneva, NY, my father moved our family to Romulus, NY in 1966. I would spend the next nine years living in that region and attending school at Romulus Central School. Having developed friendships with the students and teachers there, it felt like my life revolved around that reality. During that time my life was also being influenced by our attendance at churches in Auburn, NY and later Ithaca, NY. It was after my father became the Pastor of Our Lord's Temple COGIC, that he decided he should live in the community and in March of 1976, moved the family with the three children who still lived at home from Romulus to Ithaca. It was extremely traumatizing for me mentally and emotionally. If that happened in this day and age, I would probably have gotten therapy. However, I was required to deal with the challenges of trying to fit in at a new Junior High School which had more students than the K-12 school I had just left. Today, I am thankful for getting to say that I have friends from both schools that I remain connected to now, over 40 years later. However, what I thought was so unfair then, was actually part of the process which GOD used to get me into position for some life changing HOLY SPIRIT encounters with some of my favorite people in the world. These people would mentor me in the ways of HOLY SPIRIT, and help introduce me to the realities of GOD that my regular church attendance never would. So it is certain, that if I hadn't been forced to move to and live in Ithaca where I would finish High School at Ithaca High, I would not have been able to stay after church services on Friday nights and begin the journey of pursuing the presence of The LORD. In the process of my development, although it might have been easy to pick out the major events which could easily be designated as spiritual milestones. I have discovered that most of the events in my life that have been particularly challenging, and presented me with struggles which I couldn't explain at the time, have turned out to be significant elements of The Plan of GOD for my life. So if I begin to look at those milestones from a chronological timeline, it would proceed in this manner. I would profess my own personal faith in JESUS as CHRIST my savior at age 7, experienced the personal presence of HOLY SIRIT at age 10, I acknowledged a call to the ministry at age 14, licensed in ministry at age 16, Ordained to the world church at age 20, Pastored my first congregation at age 23, Consecrated as Bishop at age 37, Affirmed and Released an Apostle at 40. This is the life I have known. However, for most of my time spent in "The Church," I did not know GOD. I hope that sinks in….. I had undeniably accepted ESUS CHRIT as My personal Saviour at age 7. So, according to the word of GOD, I was qualified for an eternal existence in the presence of the LORD, but I did not know HIM. The church had taught me how to have church, and perform every activity of a worship service. I knew how to do the church experience well. However, I did not have an intimate experience with the Person of My GOD.

Then came the Sunday evening, when I remember reading in the Apostle Paul's New Testament letter to the believers in Philippi; Philippians chapter 3, verses 10-12. After being in ministry for approximately 32 years from the date of his conversion experience on the Damascus road, Paul writes in verse 10 of that scripture, "That I may know HIM…" The word for know in this scripture, denotes an intimate familiarity. Paul clearly understood, that it's possible to perform the activities of a faith filled Christian, and see yourself as a disciple of JESUS CHRIST, without being consistently intimate with HIM. And this is the situation, the reality in which the great majority of the church exists. They only know what they have heard their Pastor or another Minister say about GOD, without developing their own Purposeful and Personal, Passionate Pursuit of HIS Presence. How sad it is to think that most people call themselves Christians, but very often bear little or no resemblance to the Saviour and the GOD with whom they profess to be in a committed relationship. They attempt to exist, and some even attempt to operate in higher Ecclesiastical offices within the church, with no intimacy whatsoever. It creates an atmosphere where 2Timothy 3.5 becomes a reality;

"Having a form of godliness, but denying the power thereof: from such turn away."
2 Timothy 3:5 KJV

"They will act religious, but they will reject the power that could make them godly. Stay away from people like that!"
2 Timothy 3:5 NLT

"Those people will seem to be serving God. But really they refuse to accept God's power to help them. You must stay away from people like that."
2 Timothy 3:5 EASY

The unavoidable truth is that the largest majority of the Christian church is suffering from a power shortage due to a lack of an intimate relationship with GOD. A Pastoral mentor of mine, the late Bishop Otis Lockett, Sr. used to say, "What we need is an undeniable experience with the *'isness'* of GOD, which is able to sustain us through any present or future difficulty."

LORD, give us just such an experience!!! However, such an experience can only come through an intimate interaction with the reality of our GOD through HOLY SPIRIT. This experience is not automatic to our salvation. It will not come because we are diligent church attendees. Neither will it come because we are elevated to a higher position, and become known by a title. It can only be attained through the decision to commit our lives to a, "Purposeful, Powerful, Personal and Passionate Pursuit of HIS Presence."

It requires more than faithfully attending church services.

"My soul longeth, yea, even fainteth for the courts of the Lord : my heart and my flesh crieth out for the living God."
Psalms 84:2 KJV

" I long, yes, I faint with longing to enter the courts of the Lord . With my whole being, body and soul, I will shout joyfully to the living God."
Psalms 84:2 NLT

It's the activity of Prayer through which we acquire this presence and intimacy which remains. Not a momentary experience. Nor the emotional high from attending a particularly powerful worship experience. Often I have observed people who come to church, and obtain an atmospheric acquaintance with the presence of GOD from just showing up. They are genuinely affected by the atmosphere of GOD'S presence, which those who have consecrated themselves have created. However, they are unable to experience an intimate relationship with GOD, because they are satisfied with the emotional and social gratification which they have received from that weekly, sometimes as rare as monthly experience. They have no desire for more. They are content to remain one of those who when they are in attendance casually settle into an outer court experience, just an attending participant in the congregation. They are never able to define The FATHER beyond that occasional experience.

One thing that challenges me may seem a bit controversial to some. However it is not intended as a judgment or an indictment of what is most definitely, a uniquely personal experience between mankind, and a faith based experience with an Almighty GOD. But, I have challenged myself with this question; is it possible to embrace a salvation experience with the person of the Heavenly Trinity, without being fully consumed with the love of GOD? The totality of my experience with the Person of GOD, in each of HIS forms, makes it impossible for me to live outside of an all consuming intimate interaction with My GOD.

I have often asked myself, what makes me different? What is it that created my hunger for HIS presence? It's not about following a list of step by step instructions, rather it has developed from an inward desire and lingering question…. Shouldn't my relationship with GOD, be more practically relevant to my personal life outside of the church building?

I spent the majority of my life in a church which would regularly teach and preach about a religious concept of GOD. The problem is, they did almost nothing to teach me about the person of GOD. I can clearly remember a message preached by one of My God Fathers, the late Superintendant Leo Hughey, Jr. His subject was, "The Intangible Made Tangible." That was the type of revelational truth that stirred my passion to know GOD intimately.

The second reason that I pray, is because I need supernatural assistance to live successfully as a disciple of JESUS the CHRIST (The Anointed One and HIS Anointing.) I have discovered through many years of my understanding of the Christian lifestyle, and my efforts to adhere to the biblical teachings of the gospel of JESUS, that it is impossible to live that reality in my own strength. I am not intelligent enough, though I have an extremely high IQ. I am not wise enough, though I am well beyond the reality of a novice and have been to two universities, acquired several added certificates, and been in the Ecclesiastic Ministry for over 43 years. Even the added experiences of life itself are not sufficient to give me the ability to live successfully solely dependent upon my own character, and strength. I have an adversary who has existed since creation. The goal of my adversary is to disrupt GOD'S plan for my life. Defeat me in my efforts to successfully complete any and every assignment given to me by GOD; and ultimately destroy me in an attempt to prevent me from living as an example of the love and power of GOD, in my attempt to create more disciples of JESUS CHRIST. My adversary wants me to live a miserably defeated and brief existence in the earth. However, I discovered that My FATHER desires to reinforce and supersede my weaknesses and shortcomings with HIS unlimited strength. If I will receive the help which HE provides, I will never fail as I live in complete unity with HIM. (Halleluiah)

" Grace and peace be multiplied unto you through the knowledge of God, and of Jesus our Lord, According as his divine power hath given unto us all things that pertain unto life and godliness, through the knowledge of him that hath called us to glory and virtue: Whereby are given unto us exceeding great and precious promises: that by these ye might be partakers of the divine nature, having escaped the corruption that is in the world through lust. And beside this, giving all diligence, add to your faith virtue; and to virtue knowledge; And to knowledge temperance; and to temperance patience; and to patience godliness; And to godliness brotherly kindness; and to brotherly kindness charity. For if these things be in you, and abound, they make you that ye shall neither be barren nor unfruitful in the knowledge of our Lord Jesus Christ. But he that lacketh these things is blind, and cannot see afar off, and hath forgotten that he was purged from his old sins. Wherefore the

rather, brethren, give diligence to make your calling and election sure: for if ye do these things, ye shall never fall:"
2 Peter 1:2-10 KJV

" May grace (God's favor) and peace (which is perfect well-being, all necessary good, all spiritual prosperity, and freedom from fears and agitating passions and moral conflicts) be multiplied to you in [the full, personal, precise, and correct] knowledge of God and of Jesus our Lord. For His divine power has bestowed upon us all things that [are requisite and suited] to life and godliness, through the [full, personal] knowledge of Him Who called us by and to His own glory and excellence (virtue). By means of these He has bestowed on us His precious and exceedingly great promises, so that through them you may escape [by flight] from the moral decay (rottenness and corruption) that is in the world because of covetousness (lust and greed), and become sharers (partakers) of the divine nature. For this very reason, adding your diligence [to the divine promises], employ every effort in exercising your faith to develop virtue (excellence, resolution, Christian energy), and in [exercising] virtue [develop] knowledge (intelligence), And in [exercising] knowledge [develop] self-control, and in [exercising] self-control [develop] steadfastness (patience, endurance), and in [exercising] steadfastness [develop] godliness (piety), And in [exercising] godliness [develop] brotherly affection, and in [exercising] brotherly affection [develop] Christian love. For as these qualities are yours and increasingly abound in you, they will keep [you] from being idle or unfruitful unto the [full personal] knowledge of our Lord Jesus Christ (the Messiah, the Anointed One). For whoever lacks these qualities is blind, [spiritually] shortsighted, seeing only what is near to him, and has become oblivious [to the fact] that he was cleansed from his old sins. Because of this, brethren, be all the more solicitous and eager to make sure (to ratify, to strengthen, to make steadfast) your calling and election; for if you do this, you will never stumble or fall."
2 Peter 1:2-10 AMPC

"May grace and perfect peace cascade over you as you live in the rich knowledge of God and of Jesus our Lord. Everything we could ever need for life and godliness has already been deposited in us by his divine power. For all this was lavished upon us through the rich experience of knowing him who has called us by name and invited us to come to him through a glorious manifestation of his

goodness. As a result of this, he has given you magnificent promises that are beyond all price, so that through the power of these tremendous promises you can experience partnership with the divine nature, by which you have escaped the corrupt desires that are of the world. So devote yourselves to lavishly supplementing your faith with goodness, and to goodness add understanding, and to understanding add the strength of self-control, and to self-control add patient endurance, and to patient endurance add godliness, and to godliness add mercy toward your brothers and sisters, and to mercy toward others add unending love. Since these virtues are already planted deep within, and you possess them in abundant supply, they will keep you from being inactive or fruitless in your pursuit of knowing Jesus Christ more intimately. But if anyone lacks these things, he is blind, constantly closing his eyes to the mysteries of our faith, and forgetting his innocence —for his past sins have been washed away. For this reason, beloved ones, be eager to confirm and validate that God has invited you to salvation and claimed you as his own. If you do these things, you will never stumble."
2 Peter 1:2-10 TPT

"Grace and peace be given to you more and more, because you truly know God and Jesus our Lord. Jesus has the power of God, by which he has given us everything we need to live and to serve God. We have these things because we know him. Jesus called us by his glory and goodness. Through these he gave us the very great and precious promises. With these gifts you can share in God's nature, and the world will not ruin you with its evil desires. Because you have these blessings, do your best to add these things to your lives: to your faith, add goodness; and to your goodness, add knowledge; and to your knowledge, add self-control; and to your self-control, add patience; and to your patience, add service for God; and to your service for God, add kindness for your brothers and sisters in Christ; and to this kindness, add love. If all these things are in you and are growing, they will help you to be useful and productive in your knowledge of our Lord Jesus Christ. But anyone who does not have these things cannot see clearly. He is blind and has forgotten that he was made clean from his past sins. My brothers and sisters, try hard to be certain that you really are called and chosen by God. If you do all these things, you will never fall."
2 Peter 1:2-10 NCV

"May God give you more and more grace and peace as you grow in your knowledge of God and Jesus our Lord. By his divine power, God has given us everything we need for living a godly life. We have received all of this by coming to know him, the one who called us to himself by means of his marvelous glory and excellence. And because of his glory and excellence, he has given us great and precious promises. These are the promises that enable you to share his divine nature and escape the world's corruption caused by human desires. In view of all this, make every effort to respond to God's promises. Supplement your faith with a generous provision of moral excellence, and moral excellence with knowledge, and knowledge with self-control, and self-control with patient endurance, and patient endurance with godliness, and godliness with brotherly affection, and brotherly affection with love for everyone. The more you grow like this, the more productive and useful you will be in your knowledge of our Lord Jesus Christ. But those who fail to develop in this way are shortsighted or blind, forgetting that they have been cleansed from their old sins. So, dear brothers and sisters, work hard to prove that you really are among those God has called and chosen. Do these things, and you will never fall away."
2 Peter 1:2-10 NLT

Finally, quite possibly, the most important reason why I pray comes from the ultimate reason for the life, death, burial, and resurrection of JESUS. That ultimate reason is the desire to win souls and make disciples. It is a matter of my personal faith, combined with the faith of millions of other Christians throughout the world, that mankind needs a Savior. There is a need for all of humanity to choose eternal fellowship with The FATHER, or eternal separation out of HIS presence. It is the number one reason for developing a personal intimate relationship with HIM. Eternal fellowship with The FATHER is our goal. HE desires to have that relationship with each and every Human Being on this planet. It is that desire, and the spiritual requirements of making it a reality, which made it necessary for JESUS to come to the earth. The result of which is my personal salvation and redemptive experience with GOD through faith and grace allowing JESUS to become the CHRIST of my life. So, everyone who has that testimony, and can rejoice knowing that we have been given eternal access to the presence of The FATHER, has also been given another lifetime assignment. That assignment is what we also call, "The Great Commission."

"And Jesus came and spake unto them, saying, All power is given unto me in heaven and in earth. Go ye therefore, and teach all nations, baptizing them in the name of the Father, and of the Son, and of the Holy Ghost: Teaching them to observe all things whatsoever I have commanded you: and, lo, I am with you alway, even unto the end of the world. Amen."
Matthew 28:18-20 KJV

"Jesus approached and, breaking the silence, said to them, All authority (all power of rule) in heaven and on earth has been given to Me. Go then and make disciples of all the nations, baptizing them into the name of the Father and of the Son and of the Holy Spirit, Teaching them to observe everything that I have commanded you, and behold, I am with you all the days (perpetually, uniformly, and on every occasion), to the [very] close and consummation of the age. Amen (so let it be)."
Matthew 28:18-20 AMPC

"Then Jesus came close to them and said, "All the authority of the universe has been given to me. Now wherever you go, make disciples of all nations, baptizing them in the name of the Father, the Son, and the Holy Spirit. And teach them to faithfully follow all that I have commanded you. And never forget that I am with you every day, even to the completion of this age."
Matthew 28:18-20 TPT

"Then Jesus came to them and said, "All power in heaven and on earth is given to me. So go and make followers of all people in the world. Baptize them in the name of the Father and the Son and the Holy Spirit. Teach them to obey everything that I have taught you, and I will be with you always, even until the end of this age."

Matthew 28:18-20 NCV

"Jesus came and told his disciples, "I have been given all authority in heaven and on earth. Therefore, go and make disciples of all the nations, baptizing them in the name of the Father and the Son and the Holy Spirit. Teach these new disciples to obey all the commands I have given you. And be sure of this: I am with you always, even to the end of the age."
Matthew 28:18-20 NLT

There is no more powerful or pressing reason for my prayer life. Everything that I believe and every way in which I attempt to model those beliefs are a result of this commandment of JESUS. Those of us who believe in living in eternal fellowship with The FATHER are compelled to share our faith for that future with every Human Being that we can reach. The desire to fulfill the work of CHRIST JESUS given to me through the great commission has allowed me to embrace and utilize various methods of sharing the gospel of JESUS to every creature. Going everywhere and to every living person requires a commitment from us beyond just being a good church attending Christian. It also involves a strategy from HOLY SPIRIT because HE has all of the wisdom and creativity necessary to get the attention of the multitudes of people who don't always get the message in the same way as someone who might be sitting right next to them. Mark and Matthew were two of the disciples of JESUS. They were both present on the day which JESUS gave The Great Commission to HIS followers. However, they didn't both hear the words which HE spoke exactly the same ...

"And he said unto them, Go ye into all the world, and preach the gospel to every creature. He that believeth and is baptized shall be

saved; but he that believeth not shall be damned. And these signs shall follow them that believe; In my name shall they cast out devils; they shall speak with new tongues; They shall take up serpents; and if they drink any deadly thing, it shall not hurt them; they shall lay hands on the sick, and they shall recover. So then after the Lord had spoken unto them, he was received up into heaven, and sat on the right hand of God. And they went forth, and preached everywhere, the Lord working with them, and confirming the word with signs following. Amen."
Mark 16:15-20 KJV

"And He said to them, Go into all the world and preach and publish openly the good news (the Gospel) to every creature [of the whole human race]. He who believes [who adheres to and trusts in and relies on the Gospel and Him Whom it sets forth] and is baptized will be saved [from the penalty of eternal death]; but he who does not believe [who does not adhere to and trust in and rely on the Gospel and Him Whom it sets forth] will be condemned. And these attesting signs will accompany those who believe: in My name they will drive out demons; they will speak in new languages; They will pick up serpents; and [even] if they drink anything deadly, it will not hurt them; they will lay their hands on the sick, and they will get well. So then the Lord Jesus, after He had spoken to them, was taken up into heaven and He sat down at the right hand of God. [Ps. 110:1.] And they went out and preached everywhere, while the Lord kept working with them and confirming the message by the attesting signs and miracles that closely accompanied [it]. Amen (so be it)."
Mark 16:15-20 AMPC

"And he said to them, "As you go into all the world, preach openly the wonderful news of the gospel to the entire human race! Whoever believes the good news and is baptized will be saved, and whoever does not believe the good news will be condemned. And these miracle signs will accompany those who believe: They will drive out demons in the power of my name. They will speak in tongues. They will be supernaturally protected from snakes and from drinking anything poisonous. And they will lay hands on the sick and heal them." After saying these things, Jesus was lifted up into heaven and sat down at the place of honor at the right hand of God! And the apostles went out announcing the good news everywhere, as the Lord himself consistently worked with them,

validating the message they preached with miracle-signs that accompanied them!"
Mark 16:15-20 TPT

"And then he told them, "Go into all the world and preach the Good News to everyone. Anyone who believes and is baptized will be saved. But anyone who refuses to believe will be condemned. These miraculous signs will accompany those who believe: They will cast out demons in my name, and they will speak in new languages. They will be able to handle snakes with safety, and if they drink anything poisonous, it won't hurt them. They will be able to place their hands on the sick, and they will be healed." When the Lord Jesus had finished talking with them, he was taken up into heaven and sat down in the place of honor at God's right hand. And the disciples went everywhere and preached, and the Lord worked through them, confirming what they said by many miraculous signs."
Mark 16:15-20 NLT

"Jesus said to his followers, "Go everywhere in the world, and tell the Good News to everyone. Anyone who believes and is baptized will be saved, but anyone who does not believe will be punished. And those who believe will be able to do these things as proof: They will use my name to force out demons. They will speak in new languages. They will pick up snakes and drink poison without being hurt. They will touch the sick, and the sick will be healed." After the Lord Jesus said these things to his followers, he was carried up into heaven, and he sat at the right side of God. The followers went everywhere in the world and told the Good News to people, and the Lord helped them. The Lord proved that the Good News they told was true by giving them power to work miracles.]"
Mark 16:15-20 NCV

Clearly Mark heard the commandments of JESUS from a slightly different perspective than Matthew and the other two writers of the four gospels, Luke and John. So, when Mark records this account of "The Great Commission," it is worded differently than the way Matthew says it in his gospel writings. This fact also accounts for the differences in the sizes of each of the four New Testament gospel books of the HOLY BIBLE. It is all part of the same narrative, but each writer has a slightly different perspective.

That's the challenge we face when we embrace the assignments given to us in the words of JESUS found here in the books of Matthew and Mark. The larger reality is that we are called to reach out to people of varying ethnic and cultural backgrounds. Not only that, but the enemy who opposes us and the work of CHRIST in the earth, sets up issues of color, gender, sexual orientation, as well as religious, denominational, and generational doctrines in an effort to disrupt the plan of GOD.   Because of this it is imperative that we receive our instructions from the wisdom of GOD which is released to our regenerated human spirit by HOLY SPIRIT living within us. HE is so on point in the order of the operation of things that HE calls men and women from different backgrounds and differing life experiences, not in competition with one another, but to work together within a larger system of Ministry created, ordained, and anointed from Heaven to accomplish this task. Everyone who embraces and submits to this commission will hear from a slightly different perspective, and therefore preach and minister in a different way which will reach someone who is in tune with their manner of delivering the message of redemption through the blood of JESUS the CHRIST. Not only that, but HOLY SPIRIT sanctions different translations of the holy scriptures that have different names, but still represent the same power of the HOLY BIBLE released to mankind down through the ages. We live in a world with so many differences, that I am thankful for scriptural forms which allow people to hear and act upon faith as they receive the good news that JESUS is LORD!!!

And the gospel is not only limited to the speaking of the word of GOD from a pulpit. But it can also be released trough the poetry of someone like a Mother Idella Sawyer as exemplified by her Written Verse in the beginning pages of this book, works of creative arts such as Inspired Dance, Mime, Psalmist, Minstrel, and recorded songs; such as those I grew up on from the late Bishop Andrae Crouch & The Disciples, and other gospel recording artists such as The Imperials. Their music blessed and strengthened me, as well as reaching, and leading many to receive JESUS as Savior and LORD. I pray for the strength to live successfully as an example of my faith in CHRIST, and to reach those who don't know just how much The FATHER loves them.

Tell Them lyrics
by Andrae Crouch

Tell them
even if they don't believe you
Just tell them
even if they don't receive you
Oh, tell them for me
tell them for me please
please, tell them for me
tell them that i love them
And i came to let them know.

Tell them
when it seems you are forsaken

just tell them
though it seems you are earthly shaken
Oh, tell them for me
tell them for me please
please, tell them for me
tell them that i love them
And i came to let them know.

Tell that lonely man who walks
the colds streets all alone
Tell that crying child
who doesn't have a home
Tell those hungry people dying
They're lost and in despair
They don't even know that i care.

Intrumental bridge

Tell them for me please
Tell them that i love them

Oh, just tell them on the streets
and on the high ways

and tell them and even on the bi-ways
Tell them I can mend the broken heart
and restore the ones who have parted
And i came to let them know.
I came to let them know
And i came to let them know

They must know
they must know
...must know.

Lord of the Harvest

See the fields, ripe and white as snow
Up from the seeds of faith we planted long ago
So many the hearts in season
with every prayer they've grown
You have made them ready
but we must bring them home

Lord of the harvest place your fire in me
Servant you need now, servant I will be
Give me the eyes of your spirit,
your heart of compassion to know
Lord of the harvest, show me where to go

Time like a free wind, so quickly slips away
Too soon today's tomorrow, too soon yesterday
So little time for the reaping and the laborers are few
Lift your head to the fields of white
the work that you must do

Lord of the harvest place your fire in me
Servant you need now, servant I will be
Give me the eyes of your spirit,
your heart of compassion to know
Lord of the harvest, show me where to go

Wherever you may lead me
Lord of the Harvest I'll Go

Songwriters: JAMES NEWTON HOWARD / Paul Smith

Lord of the Harvest lyrics © Universal Music - Z Songs, Bridge Building get Music, Word Music LLC, Universal Music - Z Melodies, F. Hammond Music, Newton House Music, Marquis Iii Music, Universal Music-z Songs, Universal Music-z Melodies, WORD MUSIC, LLC, WORD MUSIC, INC., DAYSPRING MUSIC, LLC, EMI BLACKWOOD MUSIC INC, DAYSPRING MUSIC, INC., UNIVERSAL MUSIC-Z MELODIES OBO SCA TUNES, UNIVERSAL MUSIC-Z SONGS OBO SCA MUSIC PUBLISHING LLC, IMPERIAL MUSIC GROUP INC (MARQUIS III DIVISION)

What Is Prayer

The word pray is used 313 times in the Bible. Derivatives such as, prayed-65; prayer-114; prayers-24; prayest-2; prayeth-7; and praying-20 can also be found in the Bible. So in one form or another scripture speaks of communication between mankind and The Father 567 times, whether the word prayer is used or not. All of my life has been spent in some way related to an understanding of prayer involving a church experience. My mother gave her life to the Lord in 1960, right before I was born, and my father soon followed in 1962.

Since I was born into a churchgoing family, it's easy to understand my connection to the church having an impact on the direction of my life. However, I must confess that whereas I received a great deal of instruction within the church on what to do and what not to do, (mostly what not to do) I cannot remember a time when I was taught how to do the things that I was instructed to do. So it was with the subject of prayer. I can remember being told to pray. I can also remember a few *churchisms* such as; "If you don't pray, you won't stay;" "A little prayer, a little power; much prayer, much power." Even with that, however, more emphasis was placed upon Godly lifestyle, than was placed upon developing a personal relationship with GOD. I'll address that part of the equation more as we go forward. I remember the first time I heard someone define prayer. It was in vacation Bible school during the summer of 1968. This very nice lady at the Presbyterian Church in West Fayette,

New York said to her class that the definition of prayer is this; "Prayer is you talking to God, and God talking to you." That simple definition of prayer has stayed with me for the last 50 years of my life. Over time, and because it has been a priority of mine, I have read many books, and heard many more messages on prayer than I ever did growing up in the church. Isn't it sad that one of the most important aspects of our relationship with The FATHER received so very little emphasis in my formative years? The result of this reality was that I grew up learning how to have church well. I was good at it, so good at it, that when I was called to the ministry I was immediately set upon a fast track towards becoming a leader within the church organization. The irony of that was that I experienced the presence of GOD leading to this calling, during a time of prayer and fasting that my father, who was a Pastor by now, had urged the church to participate in. I must take a moment to confess, that while I was not taught what prayer was, or how to actively participate, I did have one of the greatest examples of just do it, that I could have ever asked for. Many nights as I grew up, I was able to observe my father in his bedroom, with the door barely cracked, on his knees before the Lord, or sitting in his chair with multiple books spread around him, as he pursued the presence and the knowledge of GOD.

So it was, at the age of 14, I can remember the first time I seriously stepped into the place of seeking GOD in prayer. I don't really know what I was expecting. However, I just wanted to be a good young man. I always knew that I was drawn to the presence of The FATHER; I just didn't know exactly how to get there. I can also plainly remember that I didn't know what to say, so I didn't say anything at all. I was just silently on my knees when I heard the voice of HOLY SPIRIT speak to me. Not only did I hear HIS voice, but in my mind, there was a bright light which accompanied the voice. It was so bright that I began to shake and I even tried to close my eyes more tightly, as if that would somehow lessen the brightness that I saw. So it was, that my very first attempt to do more than repeat a congregational prayer, or recite, "now I lay me down to sleep," resulted in the LORD informing me that HE was calling me to preach the gospel of JESUS CHRIST.

Let's be clear, I was 14 years old at the time. I was still a teenager both physically and mentally. I wasn't then, and am not now a perfect person. I often marvel at GOD'S choice to use us in spite of our imperfections. How amazing is it that GOD doesn't call the qualified, but rather qualifies the called. As a matter of fact, I still based my personal relationship with GOD primarily upon what I was not doing, and how good of a young man I was trying to be, rather than on the experience of having fellowship with a FATHER who loves me unconditionally. Outside of a few occasions shared with some of the most influential people in my life, (shout out to the Sawyer family), I was largely living on works and church doctrine. My greatest asset was the fact that I sincerely had a desire to live saved, and the fear of damaging the reputation of my father within a relatively small community. How great was and is The FATHER'S love for us, because even though I was still farther from HIS presence than I needed to be, HE still allowed HOLY SPIRIT to manifest through me from time to time in the gifts of HIS SIRIT. As I started college at Wake Forest

University in Winston Salem, NC, I found myself actively seeking the face of GOD even more than ever before. I figure it was due to being so far from home combined with the fact that even though I had breezed through High School, I was ill prepared for the disciplined atmosphere of a University experience. However, I have also come to realize that The FATHER was using these things to draw me more and more into HIS presence. HALLELUJAH!!! It was during these times and becoming exposed to a different worship atmosphere of the denomination that I had grown up experiencing; let's just say they had church differently in the south than they did in the north. I was gradually becoming more of a "son of GOD," rather than a churchgoing young man.

All of these different experiences have led me to this place in which I exist at this moment in my life. I have been blessed to experience the tangible results of prayer. It is clear that there are different definitions of prayer.

For example, the Web Bible Biblical Encyclopedia defines prayer this way:

Prayer is conversation with God; the intercourse of the soul with God, not in contemplation or meditation, but in direct address to him. Prayer may be oral or mental, occasional or constant, ejaculatory or formal. It is a "beseeching the Lord" (Ex. 32:11); "pouring out the soul before the Lord" (1 Sam. 1:15); "praying and crying to heaven" (2 Chr. 32:20); "seeking unto God and making supplication" (Job 8:5); "drawing near to God" (Ps. 73:28); "bowing the knees" (Eph. 3:14).

Prayer is frequently commanded in Scripture (Ex. 22:23, 27; 1 Kings 3:5; 2 Chr. 7:14; Ps. 37:4; Isa. 55:6; Joel 2:32; Ezek. 36:37, etc.). Pray, noun: "To ask that the laws of the universe be annulled in behalf of a single petitioner confessedly unworthy" (Ambrose Bierce, 1842-1914).

"Prayer is like the dove that Noah sent forth, which blessed him not only when it returned with an olive-leaf in its mouth, but when it never returned at all" (Robinson's Job).

Prayer presupposes a belief in the personality of GOD, his ability and willingness to communicate with us, his personal control of all things, and of all his creatures and all their actions.

What is consistent throughout the word of GOD, and the experiences of mankind, is that most people pray the prayer of petition more than any other type or form of prayer. Most only approach The FATHER on behalf of needs. Most people are like I was growing up in a church experience, we ask for a lot, but rarely say thank you. Even when we do mature enough to courteously say Thank You, we still are empty in the area of relationship. Sadly, I was taught how to have church very well. However, no one ever taught me how to go after The FATHER'S heart, or of the importance of developing an intimate personal relationship with HIM. However, I can remember in 1981, at the age of 20, I heard a song by Andrae Crouch called "I Just Want to Know You". Something happened when I heard that song. I had read Philippians 3.10, and it had stuck with me. When I heard the song written by Andrae Crouch, I was inspired to read it again. Something was alive within me. My heart was hungry for a deeper knowledge of that scripture. This time when I read it, I read the whole chapter. Over the years, I have given a great deal of time to praying and studying verses 7-16. However, it wasn't until I discovered that this letter of Paul's to Timothy and the church at Philippi was written over 32 years after his initial Damascus road experience that I laid hold upon this scripture as the driving theme of my life. It had become personal to me. I was driven from that time till now, to know HIM!

Constrained To Pray

So it was, almost 30 years later, that the FATHER allowed me to have two very significant experiences that would propel me to this assignment in my life. On February 11th, 2009 during one of my 40 day times of consecration before the FATHER, I was working third shift as a security officer at St. Francis Hospital in Greenville, South Carolina. I would think that the mere fact that I was nearing the end of 40 days of prayer and fasting, would be an indication that I was committed to a life of seeking GOD, spending time with The Father, and continually pursuing a more intimate relationship with HIM. However, that particular night, as I was listening to a praise and worship CD, I was overwhelmed by the presence of HOLY SPIRIT in my vehicle during my patrol of the campus buildings. As HE began to speak to me, HE did so very matter of factly:

HOLY SPIRIT said to me, *"Walter how is your family doing?"* It was immediately clear that we were in an intimate conversation. In these moments, I was in the midst of one of the most Defining Experiences of My life. February 11, 2009. It was two days before the end of my 40 day consecration. It was the fourth year in a row that I had done 40 Days and Nights of Seeking GOD. So when The LORD asked me how my family was doing, I knew that it was a question to which HE already knew the answer. *"You have raised your children well; your wife is capable of handling things. They may be sad if you are no longer around, but they are capable of living without you. Can they live successfully without you?"* At this point, I asked HIM, "Lord, are you getting ready to bring me home?" I had one request of GOD from my earlier days of studying the departure of the patriarchs in the Bible. That when it was time for me to transition from the earth realm, that HE would let me know in advance. Now, some of you may think that request is unrealistic. However, I personally know several people who were allowed to say goodbye to their loved ones before they departed the earth realm. Three of these people were very close to me. My mother Gloria Roberts, My Father the Reverend James T. Roberts, Sr., and my Godfather the Reverend Ernest Joseph Matthews, Jr., each of these people were able to say goodbye, and bless their loved ones prior to transitioning from earth to heaven. So it was not out of the thoughts or expectation of my reality, that I could make such a request to the LORD. And in this situation, I was wondering if HE was preparing me to leave the earth. However, in that moment, HE responded to me;

"I'm not here to bring you home Walter. I am here to let you know what is important to me about you. You are a person who will pray and spend time with ME. You have learned to preach and teach well. You have good information to share, because you spend time discerning what I have said in MY word. So, you know the difference between what I have said, and what I am saying now. So, I came to tell you that I need you in the Kingdom. But, I don't need you for your preaching or your teaching. I need you for your praying. I have many men and women who spend time making themselves better teachers and preachers of MY word. But very few, the percentage is very low on the number of MY leaders who will pray. Many of them are better able to move the people emotionally, better than you, but that is not what opens Heaven for the people. It is the prayer of MY people that opens heaven for the release of MY presence in the earth realm, and I need leaders in

the ministry of the Kingdom who will pray. So Walter, I came to let you know, that I need your praying more than I need your preaching. As a matter of fact, I want that to be the driving force and central purpose of your life here in the earth. I will give you a choice to accept MY will for your life, or live hear preparing for your transition."

So, it was an easy choice for me to embrace GOD'S will for my life. I have no higher purpose in my earthly existence, than to open Heaven continually for the manifest presence of the Kingdom of Heaven to operate freely and powerfully in this earth realm. I Live To Pray!

I have waited to share that experience for almost ten years. I have only related it a couple of times in the past few years while ministering. However, I have discovered that there are very few people who have a real hunger for the presence of GOD. HOLY SPIRIT is a constant friend in my life, and wants to be so in the life of every believer. So many people have little or no relationship with the FATHER because they don't understand the true value of knowing HIM in an intimate reality. One reason I struggled for over four years to write this book, is because I have been through so many devastating life experiences over the past few years. Each of those experiences has challenged my faith in very real ways. I have experienced the breakup of marriage, seen a cancer that I have been told is incurable take me to the point of death, and the breakup of a thriving worldwide ministry. In the midst of these experiences, people walked away from my life. Friends stopped calling me and never bothered to inquire. Church members walked away, one couple who had been very close to my family, and to whom we had given free access to our home and our children and every part of our lives, walked away, declaring that my family was no longer good ground to be connected to. For the record, they were excellent in their submission to authority, and I believe that they truly love my family to this day. However, the Bible says, out of the abundance of the heart the mouth speaks. The pain which I experienced, and in some ways continue to battle, was excruciating. Through it all, I did have the blessing of three great children who are each ordained ministers, as well as several sons and daughters in ministry who chose to stay committed to me as their Spiritual Father. Remarkably, not one of the Churches who are a part of the Global Fellowship of Ministries left the fellowship, and some more have been added. That was an encouragement to me. It let me know that there is always something good going on, even in our darkest days. So it was significant when My dear friend and one of the first two people to become partners in worldwide ministry 23 years ago, Minister Rose Shuman called in October of 2015 and encouraged me to get started writing, she didn't know the full extent of what was coming, but clearly HOLY SPIRIT was speaking through her. Finally, I said to GOD two reasons why I didn't have the energy or inspiration to write this book; first, I said that no one would read a book by someone who wasn't widely known and seemed to be irrelevant. HE said,

"Walter, as long as you are praying, you are relevant. You don't have to be seen to be relevant."

That was one objection down.

Then, I lamented to HIM, "I'm not sure that what I have to say matters." So, that's when HOLY SPIRIT shared with me, that writing this book was not about what I have to say that would matter to people, but rather what HE would be saying to people through me. There is still a mysterious aspect about my relationship with GOD, which gives me a greater desire to have my questions answered. I confess that no matter how long I have been on this journey of prayer in my life, there is still much more that I want to know, so much more to be known. So, I will never pray less. I will never think that I have arrived or learned enough. Even though I have now gone well beyond thirty two years since embracing JESUS as CHRIST and as LORD, the weight of Philippians 3.10a, "That I may know him…" still lives large within my spirit. The revelation that the Apostle Paul was inspired to write those words after having had a personal encounter with the presence of Christ on the road to Damascus 32 years prior is captivating to me.

LINGERING QUESTIONS

"He made known his ways unto Moses, his acts unto the children of Israel."
Psalms 103:7 KJV

"He revealed his plans to Moses and let the people of Israel see his mighty deeds."
Psalm 103:7 GNTD

"He made known His ways [of righteousness and justice] to Moses, His acts to the children of Israel."
Psalm 103:7 AMPC

"He revealed his character to Moses and his deeds to the people of Israel."
Psalms 103:7 NLT

"You unveiled to Moses your plans and showed Israel's sons what you could do."
Psalms 103:7 TPT

"And the Lord spake unto Moses face to face, as a man speaketh unto his friend. And he turned again into the camp: but his servant Joshua, the son of Nun, a young man, departed not out of the tabernacle."
Exodus 33:11 KJV

"And there arose not a prophet since in Israel like unto Moses, whom the Lord knew face to face,"
Deuteronomy 34:10 KJV

"No prophet ever again arose in Israel like Moses, who knew the Lord face to face."
Deuteronomy 34:10 NET

"And Enoch walked with God: and he was not; for God took him."
Genesis 5:24 KJV

"After the birth of Methuselah, Enoch lived in close fellowship with God for another 300 years, and he had other sons and daughters. Enoch lived 365 years, walking in close fellowship with God. Then one day he disappeared, because God took him."
Genesis 5:22-24 NLT

"Enoch walked [in habitual fellowship] with God after the birth of Methuselah 300 years and had other sons and daughters. So all the days of Enoch were 365 years. And Enoch walked [in habitual fellowship] with God; and he was not, for God took him [home with Him]." [Heb. 11:5.]
Genesis 5:22-24 AMPC

"After Methuselah was born, Enoch lived as God wanted for 300 years. During this time, he had other sons and daughters. Enoch lived on earth for 365 years. Enoch lived to please God all this time, then Enoch was not there any more. God took Enoch to be with him."
Genesis 5:22-24 EASY

A brief observance of the lives of Moses and Enoch can give us a revelation of the power of an intimate relationship with THE FATHER. Each of these men had a demonstrably deeper personal relationship with the GOD with whom they had established and pursued a powerfully intimate faith relationship. In the New Testament book of Hebrews, Enoch is once again mentioned as follows:

"By faith Enoch was translated that he should not see death; and was not found, because God had translated him: for before his translation he had this testimony, that he pleased God."
Hebrews 11:5 KJV

" Faith translated Enoch from this life and he was taken up into heaven! He never had to experience death; he just disappeared from this world because God promoted him. For before he was translated to the heavenly realm his life had become a pleasure to God."
Hebrews 11:5 TPT

What is clear to me now as I write this book, is that the relationship which each of these men had developed with GOD was demonstrated as an expression of the strong faith that guided their lives. But it was reading these scriptures as a young Christian which added to an already existing heart full of questions consistently affected by a desire to know more than what I could get answered by Sunday church attendance alone.

Those questions never went away. I have never considered myself to be, "deep." However, I have been told that I think, too much. I have always wondered in what way that has affected me, other than manifesting in me becoming comfortably content with spending extended periods alone. But I have discovered that my personal time alone has become a time purposefully spent in the presence of GOD. Since this book is not intended as a manual on how to pray, I have left out some things which might otherwise have been included. I am being a bit presumptuous by assuming you will know that I received the filling of HOLY SPIRIT subsequent to accepting JESUS as my personal Savior. I purposely choose to avoid an in depth discussion of that experience, because it is a subject worthy of exclusive attention in another book. However, it is absolutely imperative that I share with you, that there is no possible way that I could have then, nor continue now, to address the questions within me, without the ever present help of HOLY SPIRIT. I discovered that it has been HOLY SPIRIT all along who has fanned the flame of desire within my spirit man. This has been what has fueled my lack of satisfaction with incomplete church doctrinal teaching, and an acceptance of dispassionate expressions of the pursuit of HIS presence. I had to admit, that having a hunger for HIS presence, was, and is not the same as enjoying a regular congregational worship service. They taught me how to do church well. But they did not teach how to know HIM well. How did Mother Haines and Mother Williams know with such certainty that their Lord was, "Just like sweet honey in the rock..."? How could I know that my GOD wanted me to enter into a relationship with HIM, which would allow me access to both truths and mysteries? A relationship which was available to all was seemingly pursued by so very few. Why didn't my original mentors and fathers teach me these things? Why is it, that my personal observation of more than what was usually experienced in a church service come so rarely, and was seemingly manifested by only certain individuals? It was also those certain individuals, such as my God Father Elder Ernest J. Matthews, Jr who because of their demonstrated relationship with HIS presence, who were considered radical and dangerous. All people who demonstrated the same qualities were exceptions. I don't blame the denomination which I grew up in, and still admire to this day. What I believe is that people throughout the church all around the world, easily fall into the deception that church attendance and membership is the same as having an intimate relationship with GOD. This is clearly not the truth. Another point that is necessary to make, is that this kind of intimate relationship with GOD does not come from extensive knowledge or theological study.

"Not that we are sufficient of ourselves to think any thing as of ourselves; but our sufficiency is of God; Who also hath made us able ministers of the new testament; not of the letter, but of the spirit: for the letter killeth, but the spirit giveth life."
2 Corinthians 3:5-6 KJV

"Not that we are fit (qualified and sufficient in ability) of ourselves to form personal judgments or to claim or count anything as coming from us, but our power and ability and sufficiency are from God. [It is He] Who has qualified us [making us to be fit and worthy and sufficient] as ministers and dispensers of a new covenant [of salvation through Christ], not [ministers] of the letter (of legally written code) but of the Spirit; for the code [of the Law] kills, but the [Holy] Spirit makes alive." [Jer. 31:31.]
2 Corinthians 3:5-6 AMPC

"Yet we don't see ourselves as capable enough to do anything in our own strength, for our true competence flows from God's empowering presence . He alone makes us adequate ministers who are focused on an entirely new covenant. Our ministry is not based on the letter of the law but through the power of the Spirit. The letter of the law kills, but the Spirit pours out life."
2 Corinthians 3:5-6 TPT

"God has made us his servants. So we are able to tell people the message of his new agreement . This new agreement is not about rules. Rules tell people what they must do and they bring death. But God's new agreement comes from his Spirit . And the Spirit brings new life to us, not death."

2 Corinthians 3:6 EASY

I needed to discover another way to find what I was searching for. What happened to me and for me was my personal experience which was driven by the presence of HOLY SPIRIT in my life. I would occasionally come across scriptures which would motivate me to discover what they meant. I can remember one of my Theology professors at Wake Forest University saying in class one day, "The Bible says what it says, and it means what it means. Our responsibility is to try and discern what it means by what it says." I have never forgotten that statement. While I am certain that there are specific meanings, and truths to be discerned within the scripture, I am also certain that there are meanings and truths which can only be revealed with the assistance of HOLY SPIRIT. So, I would have experiences in the study of the scripture when I would read something which would grab my attention.

"But if from thence thou shalt seek the Lord thy God, thou shalt find him, if thou seek him with all thy heart and with all thy soul."
Deuteronomy 4:29 KJV

" But if from there you will seek (inquire for and require as necessity) the Lord your God, you will find Him if you [truly] seek Him with all your heart [and mind] and soul and life."
Deuteronomy 4:29 AMPC

"But even then, if you look for the Lord your God, you will find him. You must really want to find him. If you do, you will certainly find him."
Deuteronomy 4:29 EASY

"And thou, Solomon my son, know thou the God of thy father, and serve him with a perfect heart and with a willing mind: for the Lord searcheth all hearts, and understandeth all the imaginations of the thoughts: if thou seek him, he will be found of thee; but if thou forsake him, he will cast thee off for ever."
1 Chronicles 28:9 KJV

"And you, Solomon my son, know the God of your father [have personal knowledge of Him, be acquainted with, and understand Him; appreciate, heed, and cherish Him] and serve Him with a blameless heart and a willing mind. For the Lord searches all hearts and minds and understands all the wanderings of the thoughts. If you seek Him [inquiring for and of Him and requiring Him as your first and vital necessity] you will find Him; but if you forsake Him, He will cast you off forever!"
1 Chronicles 28:9 AMPC

"And Solomon, my son, learn to know the God of your ancestors intimately. Worship and serve him with your whole heart and a willing mind. For the Lord sees every heart and knows every plan and thought. If you seek him, you will find him. But if you forsake him, he will reject you forever."
1 Chronicles 28:9 NLT

"'And you, Solomon my son, know your father's God. Be his faithful servant in every way with your whole mind. The Lord knows what you are thinking. And he understands all your thoughts. If you look for him, you will find him. But if you leave him, he will turn away from you for all time."
1 Chronicles 28:9 EASY

"For through him we both have access by one Spirit unto the Father."
Ephesians 2:18 KJV

"For it is through Him that we both [whether far off or near] now have an introduction (access) by one [Holy] Spirit to the Father [so that we are able to approach Him]."

Ephesians 2:18 AMPC

"Now all of us can come to the Father through the same Holy Spirit because of what Christ has done for us."
Ephesians 2:18 NLT

"Now we all have received the same Holy Spirit , because of what Christ has done for us. As a result, we can all come near to God the Father."
Ephesians 2:18 EASY

"And now, because we are united to Christ, we both have equal and direct access in the realm of the Holy Spirit to come before the Father!"
Ephesians 2:18 TPT

"In whom we have boldness and access with confidence by the faith of him."
Ephesians 3:12 KJV

"Because of Christ and our faith in him, we can now come boldly and confidently into God's presence."
Ephesians 3:12 NLT

"In Whom, because of our faith in Him, we dare to have the boldness (courage and confidence) of free access (an unreserved approach to God with freedom and without fear)."
Ephesians 3:12 AMPC

"Because we are united with Christ, we can come near to God. We are not afraid to do that. We can be sure that God will accept us, because we trust in Christ."
Ephesians 3:12 EASY

"we have boldness through him, and free access as kings before the Father because of our complete confidence in Christ's faithfulness".

Ephesians 3:12 TPT

"Let us draw near with a true heart in full assurance of faith, having our hearts sprinkled from an evil conscience, and our bodies washed with pure water."
Hebrews 10:22 KJV

"we come closer to God and approach him with an open heart, fully convinced that nothing will keep us at a distance from him. For our hearts have been sprinkled with blood to remove impurity, and we have been freed from an accusing conscience. Now we are clean, unstained, and presentable to God inside and out!"
Hebrews 10:22 TPT

"Let us all come forward and draw near with true (honest and sincere) hearts in unqualified assurance and absolute conviction engendered by faith (by that leaning of the entire human personality on God in absolute trust and confidence in His power, wisdom, and goodness), having our hearts sprinkled and purified from a guilty (evil) conscience and our bodies cleansed with pure water."
Hebrews 10:22 AMPC

"By his death, Jesus opened a new and life-giving way through the curtain into the Most Holy Place. And since we have a great High Priest who rules over God's house, let us go right into the presence of God with sincere hearts fully trusting him. For our guilty consciences have been sprinkled with Christ's blood to make us clean, and our bodies have been washed with pure water."
Hebrews 10:20-22 NLT

Over and over again, when I would come across these scriptures, I would be motivated to get closer. Finally, the real spark came when I read a somewhat common passage of scripture spoken often in our church...

"But he giveth more grace. Wherefore he saith, God resisteth the proud, but giveth grace unto the humble. Submit yourselves

therefore to God. Resist the devil, and he will flee from you. Draw nigh to God, and he will draw nigh to you. Cleanse your hands, ye sinners; and purify your hearts, ye double minded."
James 4:6-8 KJV

Somehow it seemed, too simple, too easy to be true. So, finally I found a key that would change my life my forever. I found myself sensing the presence of GOD more frequently. Suddenly, I would hear a "sound," a voice speaking to me, calling to me, that I hadn't heard during the testimony service. I didn't hear it when the choir was singing. I didn't hear it when the Pastor was preaching. I found myself gladly going to the altar whenever the opportunity was offered. I just wanted to sense that presence. I was anxious to hear that "sound," that voice and sense that intimacy. I felt like every time at the altar was an opportunity to experience something new and fresh. How good is GOD, it was as if HE knew that I needed help. Our Church Mother Idella Sawyer's adult children would begin to stay at the church on Friday nights after the service was over. I think that my father allowed me to stay, because my older sister Janice who currently Pastors along with her husband James Teasley, was staying as well. It was Mother Sawyer's son Csiko (Pastor of Oasis Fellowship in Ithaca, NY) his wife Loraine Rashida and Mother Sawyer's daughter Jaqueline who had the greatest influence on me during that time of my life. Later Rod Wilson would become a member of our church group. Rod and I would later be ordained in the same service on August 23, 1981. Through those Friday night times of lingering in his presence, singing would become worship, and worship would become waiting in HIS presence; praying in The SPIRIT, until tangible manifestation would be present within our midst. HALLELUJAH!!!

What happened to me was sparked by the things which I learned through my experiences with a small group of about six people who just decided to hang around seeking more.

SEEKING MORE

That is how it began. I had then, and still have now, an unquenchable desire for more. Attending church services were ok, but there's nothing like that first time I experienced HIS voice for myself. I had progressed from longing for the presence of the LORD, to a great anticipation of hearing HIS voice. The more I stayed in HIS presence, the more I grew to expect a tangible manifestation of HIS presence. I wanted to hear that sound. I began to realize that the LORD is always speaking, but we do not always position ourselves to hear what HE wants to say to us. Most Christians only see prayer, as a time for asking GOD for the things they want. They also plead for HIS help when they are in trouble. How sad it is that getting to know the heart of The FATHER is an experience that only few take advantage of.

> "To the praise of the glory of his grace, wherein he hath made us accepted in the beloved."
> Ephesians 1:6 KJV

Few people embrace the revelation of GOD freely opening HIS presence to us, giving us access to HIM, making us accepted. All we have to do is come into HIS presence through an entrance that was opened wide for us, by the sacrifice of JESUS. I continually stop to absorb the reality of that truth. GOD loves us so much, that HE came in agreement with HIS Son JESUS, to lay down HIS life so that GOD'S earthly Sons could once again have access to all of the benefits which the FATHER GOD has to offer us; and most Christians never spend time with HIM to discover for themselves how wonderful those benefits are. I watched throughout my years in the church, loving people limit their experience with GOD to just what takes place on Sunday morning. In my case, our denomination had a Tuesday night, and Friday night service. But, the individual churches would schedule programs to spend more time on Sundays to keep the church members occupied, and to raise as much money as possible to help cover the financial needs. How wonderful it is to be able to express the freedom which I experience on a daily and moment by moment basis, knowing that the presence of GOD is with me constantly. In strictly theological terms, we experience HIS constant presence through the person of HOLY SPIRIT. It is HOLY SPIRIT who fills us, through an experience subsequent to our acceptance of JESUS CHRIST as our Lord and Savior. HE is actively urging us to pursue a more intimate relationship with The FATHER. That's what was happening to me on those Friday nights after the regular church service had ended. I was more excited about that time, than I was during the other part of the services. Truthfully, the teaching that I received during those years was a balance for me in my personal Christian development. It was like having to go to class in order to participate in High School sports. I didn't mind enduring the service, as long as I could get to the fun part.

That's right, seeking GOD and experiencing the presence of HOLY SPIRIT was the fun part. Don't misunderstand me; I didn't take the church service and the worship of GOD lightly. Rather I have always had an immense reverence for HIS awesome presence. So much so, that the opportunity to experience that presence is the very reason I pray. It didn't take long to discover that seeking HIM, led to finding HIM. I had to make the effort. I need to say that again, I needed to make the effort! Unfortunately, that is why most Christians, and even some church leaders, and Pastors, don't pray. Prayer requires an effort on our part. GOD has made HIMSELF available to us, and most church going Christians, don't make the effort.

"And Moses took the tabernacle, and pitched it without the camp, afar off from the camp, and called it the Tabernacle of the congregation. And it came to pass, that every one which sought the Lord went out unto the tabernacle of the congregation, which was without the camp. And it came to pass, when Moses went out unto the tabernacle, that all the people rose up, and stood every man at his tent door, and looked after Moses, until he was gone into the tabernacle. And it came to pass, as Moses entered into the tabernacle, the cloudy pillar descended, and stood at the door of the tabernacle, and the Lord talked with Moses. And all the people saw the cloudy pillar stand at the tabernacle door: and all the people rose up and worshipped, every man in his tent door. And the Lord spake unto Moses face to face, as a man speaketh unto his friend. And he turned again into the camp: but his servant

Joshua, the son of Nun, a young man, departed not out of the tabernacle."
Exodus 33:7-11 KJV

All GOD has ever wanted HIS people to do is make an effort. What do you want to know? Don't you have any questions? If your Pastor has answered all of your questions in your Christian life, then you have no idea just how big our GOD is. That was what drove me to pray as I grew up and developed a deeper relationship with GOD. There have always been things that I wanted to know.

"Call unto me, and I will answer thee, and shew thee great and mighty things, which thou knowest not."
Jeremiah 33:3 KJV

"Ask me and I will tell you remarkable secrets you do not know about things to come."
Jeremiah 33:3 NLT

"Call to Me and I will answer you and show you great and mighty things, fenced in and hidden, which you do not know (do not distinguish and recognize, have knowledge of and understand)."
Jeremiah 33:3 AMPC

"'Judah, pray to me, and I will answer you. I will tell you important secrets you have never heard before.'"
Jeremiah 33:3 NCV

"This is God's Message, the God who made earth, made it livable and lasting, known everywhere as God : 'Call to me and I will answer you. I'll tell you marvelous and wondrous things that you could never figure out on your own."
Jeremiah 33:2-3 MSG

The greatest of all, is the desire to know HIM. I never wanted to be an ordinary person. I always felt that I was born to be different, born to make a difference. How amazing for me to discover that GOD had arranged a way for me to get my questions answered. All I had to do was make the effort. The children of Israel were content to be led, and to follow, most of them anyway. There were some who wanted to lead, but were unwilling to pay the price to position themselves for leadership. Clearly that fact exists today as well. But, when I began seeking HIS presence; seeking the face of God, I wasn't thinking about a position of leadership. I wasn't even thinking about being called into service in the Kingdom as a Minister. I was inquisitive, and mostly I was spiritually hungry. Church services were insufficient. I soon discovered that I could have a more fulfilling worship experience, after it was combined with my personal time spent with GOD. HE has always been more than willing to share with me, anything that is available to know concerning My relationship with HIM, if I would be willing to do more than stand in the door of my tent watching as others hungrier for HIS presence went into the Tabernacle. I needed to go to the place of HIS presence, draw near to HIM. There is an available presence awaiting us when we come out of our place of comfort, come out of the tent, run to the tabernacle and worship HIM. My tabernacle is a private place where I can spend time with HIM. It doesn't have to be inside the church. I just need to make it about HIM. This really isn't a difficult process. HE is where HE is, and we just need to get there. One person once told me that I was just different. However, I found out that HOLY SPIRIT wasn't any different in sharing me, than HE is with anyone else. Every person has the same opportunity. However, I have discovered that most Christians are just lazy when it comes to prayer. As long as they have their basic necessities met, and their loved ones are safe and healthy, they don't feel compelled to pray. Staying within their tent is much more comfortable. I pray out of desire, not out of need. My time spent in the presence of GOD is a time of discovery. I am on a quest to know HIS ways more than I know HIS acts. Once prayer became a desire for me, it wasn't long before prayer became a character trait in my life. I pray all the time.

"And he spake a parable unto them to this end, that men ought always to pray, and not to faint;"
Luke 18:1 KJV

"ALSO [Jesus] told them a parable to the effect that they ought always to pray and not to turn coward (faint, lose heart, and give up)."
Luke 18:1 AMPC

"He then told them a parable on the need for them to pray always and not become discouraged:"
Luke 18:1 HCSB

"Jesus was telling them a parable about their need to pray continuously and not to be discouraged."
Luke 18:1 CEB

"Then Jesus told his disciples a parable to teach them that they should always pray and never become discouraged."
Luke 18:1 GNTD

"He told them a parable to illustrate that it is necessary always to pray and not lose heart."

Luke 18:1 MEV

"Then Jesus used this story to teach his followers that they should always pray and never lose hope."
Luke 18:1 NCV

"One day Jesus taught the apostles to keep praying and never stop or lose hope. He shared with them this illustration:"
Luke 18:1 TPT

This instruction from JESUS is so important that the Apostle Paul picks it up in his letter to Timothy and says it this way:

"Therefore, I encourage the men to pray on every occasion with hands lifted to God in worship with clean hearts, free from frustration or strife."
1 Timothy 2:8 TPT

"I desire therefore that in every place men should pray, without anger or quarreling or resentment or doubt [in their minds], lifting up holy hands."
1 Timothy 2:8 AMPC

"I will therefore that men pray every where, lifting up holy hands, without wrath and doubting."
1 Timothy 2:8 KJV

"In every place of worship, I want men to pray with holy hands lifted up to God, free from anger and controversy."
1 Timothy 2:8 NLT

David understood the intense necessity of going into HIS presence in the Psalms:

"Let my prayer be set forth before thee as incense; and the lifting up of my hands as the evening sacrifice."
Psalms 141:2 KJV

So then, what definition will I give to prayer? For me, in its purest form, prayer is equivalent to seeking GOD, making the effort to enter in to HIS presence and commune with His awesome spiritual reality. I live for this. I live to go after HIM, draw close to HIM. I hunger for HIM, I thirst for HIM. I find that the descriptions which David sang of in the Psalms are a great way to describe my constant longing, and joyful quest for the presence of the One Living and All Encompassing GOD. I learned that not only has HE made HIMSELF available and accessible, HE also looks forward to the times of unrestricted fellowship with HIS children. Oh how wonderfully awesome it is to get to know HIM. As BIG as HE is, HE becomes intimately and personally attached to us as individually valuable within HIS heart.

"O God, thou art my God; early will I seek thee: my soul thirsteth for thee, my flesh longeth for thee in a dry and thirsty land, where no water is;"
Psalms 63:1 KJV

Writing this book has become an act of personal worship for me. I find that I continually get caught up in the presence of HOLY SPIRIT as I attempt to share my journey to develop an intimate, passionate relationship with GOD. I live to pray is a truth that is an undeniable part of who I am. The only way to understand heavenly spiritual truths is to submit ourselves to the power and activity of HOLY

SPIRIT within us as HE guides us along our lifelong journey to learn and grow as children of GOD.

These things and so much more, explain why I pray. I got here by the divine arrangement of GOD, who gave me a mother that took my brother Tommy and I along with her to noon day prayer. This same GOD allowed me to have an encounter that Mother Haines and Mother Williams sang about. Those Mothers were sure and certain in their description of HIM. When they said that having an experience with GOD was just like sweet honey in the rock, they clearly sang from personal experience. What a wonderfully arranged plan of GOD, allowing me to have those Friday night experiences in times of purposeful worship; seeking HIS presence, and expecting to receive from HIM. Willingly and joyfully I was learning through personal experience the ways of GOD. I was blessed to experience active interaction with HOLY SPIRIT. I need this activity in my life. I discovered that I can know more about GOD, and not be confined to the building we call church. Rather, wherever I am, HE is there as well. From these experiences, I was propelled into a life from which there is no going back. I invite you to become an active participant in experiencing the fullness of GOD. Come out of your tent door, and join me in the place where the cloud dwells, the Tabernacle of the Congregation. It is also important for me to state here how thankful for the church. The experiences and teaching I received provided the foundation for the hunger which motivated me to seek even more. No one should ever think that I didn't and don't need the church. The Bible supports the church and commands our fellowship with other believers. It is through properly ordered fellowship that we embrace the presence of God in the lives of others and experience HIS power in operation through HOLY SPIRIT'S corporate manifestations within the Sanctuary.

"Not forsaking the assembling of ourselves together, as the manner of some is; but exhorting one another: and so much the more, as ye see the day approaching."
Hebrews 10:25 KJV

"Some people have given up the habit of meeting for worship, but we must not do that. We should keep on encouraging each other, especially since you know that the day of the Lord's coming is getting closer."
Hebrews 10:25 CEV

"Some people have stopped meeting with the group of Christians. But that is not good. We should all continue to meet together. We need to help one another to be strong and brave. That is now even more important, because the Lord's great day is coming. You know that the Lord will return soon."
Hebrews 10:25 EASY

"This is not the time to pull away and neglect meeting together, as some have formed the habit of doing. In fact, we should come together even more frequently, eager to encourage and urge each other onward as we anticipate that day dawning."
Hebrews 10:25 TPT

What I pray is that we who call ourselves "Christians," who claim to be Disciples of Jesus Christ, would recognize the need for a residing habitation of HIS presence. I pray that we will not allow ourselves to be satisfied with an occasional visitation experience in the church service. To make it a reality requires us to have a Personal and Purposeful, Passionate Pursuit of His Presence. Knowing that time spent with Our GOD will be Powerful.

Apostle Walter Roberts

PART 2

IT'S TIME TO PRAY

"I strongly suspect that if we saw all the difference even the tiniest of our prayers make, and all the people those little prayers were destined to affect, and all the consequences of those prayers down through the centuries, we would be so paralyzed with awe at the power of prayer that we would be unable to get up off our knees for the rest of our lives."
Dr. Peter Kreeft, Professor of Philosophy, Boston College

Chapter 1

ALL Kinds of PRAYER

Ephesians 6.18

"Praying always with all prayer and supplication in the Spirit, and watching thereunto with all perseverance and supplication for all saints"
Ephesians 6:18 KJV

"Pray at all times (on every occasion, in every season) in the Spirit, with all [manner of] prayer and entreaty. To that end keep alert and watch with strong purpose and perseverance, interceding in behalf of all the saints (God's consecrated people)."
Ephesians 6:18 AMPC

"Pray in the Spirit at all times with all kinds of prayers, asking for everything you need. To do this you must always be ready and never give up. Always pray for all God's people."
Ephesians 6:18 NCV

"Embrace the power of salvation's full deliverance, like a helmet to protect your thoughts from lies . And take the mighty razor-sharp Spirit-sword of the spoken Word of God. Pray passionately in the Spirit, as you constantly intercede with every form of prayer at all times. Pray the blessings of God upon all his believers."
Ephesians 6:17-18 TPT

All Prayer………..All kinds of Prayers…….. Every Form of prayer…….. Every Manner of Prayer and entreaty. Prayer does not look the same, sound the same, or feel the same for everyone. That's okay. GOD is capable of adjusting to us and the differences about us. So what matters most is that we PRAY!!! If we are Christians or Disciples of JESUS CHRIST and living a life in fellowship with the FATHER GOD, HE has an expectation of those who have this relationship with HIM that we will pray. Not might pray, but that we will pray. In almost every translation or version of the scripture, in Matthew 6.5-18, JESUS says, "When you pray…" I just happen to like the way The Passion Translation here:

"Whenever you pray, be sincere and not like the pretenders who love the attention they receive while praying before others in the meetings and on street corners. Believe me, they've already received in full their reward. But whenever you pray, go into your innermost chamber and be alone with Father God, praying to him in secret. And your Father, who sees all you do, will reward you openly. When you pray, there is no need to repeat empty phrases, praying like those who don't know God, for they expect God to hear them because of their many words. There is no need to imitate them, since your Father already knows what you need before you ask him. Pray like this: 'Our Father, dwelling in the heavenly realms, may the glory of your name be the center on which our lives turn. Manifest your kingdom realm, and cause your every purpose to be fulfilled on earth, just as it is fulfilled in heaven. We acknowledge you as our Provider of all we need each day. Forgive us the wrongs we have done as we ourselves release forgiveness to those who have wronged us. Rescue us every time we face tribulation and set us free from evil. For you are the King who rules with power and glory forever. Amen.' " And when you pray , make sure you forgive the faults of others so that your Father in heaven will also forgive you. But if you withhold forgiveness from others, your Father withholds forgiveness from you." "When you fast, don't look like those who pretend to be spiritual. They want everyone to know they're fasting, so they appear in public looking miserable, gloomy, and disheveled. Believe me, they've already received their

reward in full. When you fast, don't let it be obvious, but instead, wash your face and groom yourself and realize that your Father in the secret place is the one who is watching all that you do in secret and will continue to reward you openly."
Matthew 6:5-18 TPT

Prayer's greatest requirement is a true heart in search of the grace of GOD. As I will discuss further in this book.

"Let us draw near with a true heart in full assurance of faith, having our hearts sprinkled from an evil conscience, and our bodies washed with pure water."
Hebrews 10:22 KJV

"…we come closer to God and approach him with an open heart, fully convinced that nothing will keep us at a distance from him. For our hearts have been sprinkled with blood to remove impurity, and we have been freed from an accusing conscience. Now we are clean, unstained, and presentable to God inside and out!"
Hebrews 10:22 TPT

"Let us all come forward and draw near with true (honest and sincere) hearts in unqualified assurance and absolute conviction engendered by faith (by that leaning of the entire human personality on God in absolute trust and confidence in His power, wisdom, and goodness), having our hearts sprinkled and purified from a guilty (evil) conscience and our bodies cleansed with pure water."
Hebrews 10:22 AMPC

Getting people to pray involves two major issues for me. The first is the fact that all people need to know that I believe and hope that they do, that the GOD whom we choose to fellowship with, is able to handle all of the individual and unique differences of the people who approach HIM desiring HIS attention. The next is that though there may be biblical and doctrinal differences in the views on the effectiveness of different forms of prayer, any difference which exists should not prevent us from believing in GOD'S desire to interact with us. Do not allow your mind to override the desire of your spirit to communicate with GOD. Don't over think this reality; just pray!

We live in a world society in which our lives are continuously bombarded by interactive elements which have an effect on our minds, and are designed to influence our thought patterns and control our decisions. These elements can be positive or negative. Often that determination depends upon the familial and societal realities of our upbringing. It is because of the forces at work during my individual upbringing that I have become the man that I am. Clearly those forces which initially impacted me have been modified by the environmental elements to which I have been exposed throughout my lifetime. Therefore, I am able to make a determination on the level of effectiveness which these elements have had on my life. Because I am a University educated Sociologist, Philosopher, and Minister, spending over 50 years dealing with people in society, I am able to conclude that the greatest influence on my personal choices in life has been the continual access I have had with the presence of GOD through prayer. No other single element of my personal experiences in this world has had more effect on the man that I am, and also empowered my attempts to influence the lives of millions of other people throughout the world, hopefully for the better, than prayer.

I am not writing this book for personal satisfaction. I am writing this book from an overwhelming desire to empower the lives of people. Whether people belong to a church or not, whether they have had a personal faith relationship with GOD or not, whether they are college educated or not. My desire is to let people know that the GOD of my life, the Christian GOD of the Holy Scriptures, is ready at all times to receive and respond to all people when they pray.

FATHER, I ask that whoever obtains this book, will find a reason and take the time to pray. I ask you, by your grace, meet them at the place of their need. Make "I AM that I AM," known to them, and impact their life for the good. Let them never be the same again, better than they have ever been, in JESUS' Name; AMEN.

I have read many different books on different types and forms of prayer. In the future, I may even write another book on a specific type of prayer. However, for the purpose of this book I want to give examination to different types of prayer, but I will go into more depth with some types or forms of prayer more than others. This should not be construed as my support for any one form of prayer over another. Most likely it will be more of an indication of my current activities and focus during times spent in fellowship with The FATHER.

Chapter 2

Prayer of Petition

"And whatsoever ye shall ask in my name, that will I do, that the Father may be glorified in the Son. If ye shall ask any thing in my name, I will do it."
John 14:13-14 KJV

"And I will do [I Myself will grant] whatever you ask in My Name [as presenting all that I AM], so that the Father may be glorified and extolled in (through) the Son. [Exod. 3:14.] [Yes] I will grant [I Myself will do for you] whatever you shall ask in My Name [as presenting all that I AM]."
John 14:13-14 AMPC

"You can ask for anything in my name, and I will do it, so that the Son can bring glory to the Father. Yes, ask me for anything in my name, and I will do it!"
John 14:13-14 NLT

"For I will do whatever you ask me to do when you ask me in my name. And that is how the Son will show what the Father is really like and bring glory to him. Ask me anything in my name, and I will do it for you!"
John 14:13-14 TPT

" And in that day ye shall ask me nothing. Verily, verily, I say unto you, Whatsoever ye shall ask the Father in my name, he will give it you. Hitherto have ye asked nothing in my name: ask, and ye shall receive, that your joy may be full."
John 16:23-24 KJV

"At that time you won't need to ask me for anything. I tell you the truth, you will ask the Father directly, and he will grant your request because you use my name. You haven't done this before. Ask, using my name, and you will receive, and you will have abundant joy."
John 16:23-24 NLT

"And when that time comes, you will ask nothing of Me [you will need to ask Me no questions]. I assure you, most solemnly I tell you, that My Father will grant you whatever you ask in My Name [as presenting all that I AM]. [Exod. 3:14.] Up to this time you have not asked a [single] thing in My Name [as presenting all that I AM]; but now ask and keep on asking and you will receive, so that your joy (gladness, delight) may be full and complete."
John 16:23-24 AMPC

"For here is eternal truth: When that time comes you won't need to ask me for anything, but instead you will go directly to the Father and ask him for anything you desire and he will give it to you, because of your relationship with me. Until now you've not been bold enough to ask the Father for a single thing in my name, but now you can ask, and keep on asking him! And you can be sure that you'll receive what you ask for, and your joy will have no limits!"
John 16:23-24 TPT

"Be careful for nothing; but in every thing by prayer and supplication with thanksgiving let your requests be made known unto God."
Philippians 4:6 KJV

"Don't be pulled in different directions or worried about a thing. Be saturated in prayer throughout each day, offering your faith-filled requests before God with overflowing gratitude. Tell him every detail of your life,"
Philippians 4:6 TPT

"Do not fret or have any anxiety about anything, but in every circumstance and in everything, by prayer and petition (definite requests), with thanksgiving, continue to make your wants known to God."

Philippians 4:6 AMPC

"Do not worry about anything. Instead, pray to God about everything. Ask him to help you with the things that you need. And thank him for his help."
Philippians 4:6 EASY

"Don't worry about anything; instead, pray about everything. Tell God what you need, and thank him for all he has done."
Philippians 4:6 NLT

"And this is the confidence that we have in him, that, if we ask any thing according to his will, he heareth us: And if we know that he hear us, whatsoever we ask, we know that we have the petitions that we desired of him."
1 John 5:14-15 KJV

"And we are confident that he hears us whenever we ask for anything that pleases him. And since we know he hears us when we make our requests, we also know that he will give us what we ask for."
1 John 5:14-15 NLT

"And this is the confidence (the assurance, the privilege of boldness) which we have in Him: [we are sure] that if we ask anything (make any request) according to His will (in agreement with His own plan), He listens to and hears us. And if (since) we [positively] know that He listens to us in whatever we ask, we also know [with settled and absolute knowledge] that we have [granted us as our present possessions] the requests made of Him."
1 John 5:14-15 AMPC

"Also, we can really trust God to help us when we turn to him. We know that he will hear us. When we ask for anything that he wants us to have, he listens to us. Since we know that, we also know that God will give to us the things that we ask for. It is like we have already received those things from him."

1 John 5:14-15 EASY

"Since we have this confidence, we can also have great boldness before him, for if we ask anything agreeable to his will, he will hear us. And if we know that he hears us in whatever we ask, we also know that we have obtained the requests we ask of him."
1 John 5:14-15 TPT

By definition, a petition can be a noun or a verb. For the purpose of this book, I will define both.

A petition is a request which is made of one who has the authority and ability to grant a request. It is also the activity of making the request of an authority which is able to grant it. So then, as a noun we can make our petition to THE FATHER Whom we believe by faith, has the Authority and the Ability to grant our request. We can also actively compel by our appealing to THE FATHER to grant our request. It is the activity of approaching HIM, and appealing to HIS characteristics of love, mercy, kindness, compassion, justice, fairness, favor, longsuffering, and goodness, which is the act of petitioning HIM in order to get a positive response. This activity would take the form of a verb.

The prayer of petition is without a doubt, the most often used form of prayer. The Bible doesn't just tell us to ask GOD, making our requests to HIM; but it also instructs in the details of asking. The Bible also challenges our expectation, telling us that we should expect to receive an answer to prayer, or a granted petition request. We ask because we hold the expectation that HE will receive our petition and answer our requests. Does HE exist? Is

HE real? Am I qualified to approach HIM? Does HE hear me? If HE hears me, will HE answer my prayer?

" But without faith it is impossible to please him: for he that cometh to God must believe that he is, and that he is a rewarder of them that diligently seek him."
Hebrews 11:6 KJV

" But without faith it is impossible to please and be satisfactory to Him. For whoever would come near to God must [necessarily] believe that God exists and that He is the rewarder of those who earnestly and diligently seek Him [out]."
Hebrews 11:6 AMPC

"And it is impossible to please God without faith. Anyone who wants to come to him must believe that God exists and that he rewards those who sincerely seek him."
Hebrews 11:6 NLT

"But without faith no one can please God. We must believe that God is real and rewards everyone who searches for him."
Hebrews 11:6 CEV

So, what is the condition of our faith? Do we have faith to believe? Why would we take the time and make the effort to pray to GOD unless we believe that HE exists? Because, if we don't believe that GOD even exists, then we would be wasting our time and making a clearly futile physical attempt to get the attentions of an unknown Spiritual being.   Thankfully, GOD does exist, and longs to bless HIS people.

" I sought the Lord , and he heard me, and delivered me from all my fears. They looked unto him, and were lightened: and their faces were not ashamed. This poor man cried, and the Lord heard him, and saved him out of all his troubles. The angel of the Lord

encampeth round about them that fear him, and delivereth them. O taste and see that the Lord is good: blessed is the man that trusteth in him. O fear the Lord , ye his saints: for there is no want to them that fear him. The young lions do lack, and suffer hunger: but they that seek the Lord shall not want any good thing."
Psalms 34:4-10 KJV

" I sought (inquired of) the Lord and required Him [of necessity and on the authority of His Word], and He heard me, and delivered me from all my fears. [Ps. 73:25; Matt. 7:7.] They looked to Him and were radiant; their faces shall never blush for shame or be confused. This poor man cried, and the Lord heard him, and saved him out of all his troubles. The Angel of the Lord encamps around those who fear Him [who revere and worship Him with awe] and each of them He delivers. [Ps. 18:1; 145:20.] O taste and see that the Lord [our God] is good! Blessed (happy, fortunate, to be envied) is the man who trusts and takes refuge in Him. [I Pet. 2:2, 3.] O fear the Lord, you His saints [revere and worship Him]! For there is no want to those who truly revere and worship Him with godly fear. The young lions lack food and suffer hunger, but they who seek (inquire of and require) the Lord [by right of their need and on the authority of His Word], none of them shall lack any beneficial thing."
Psalm 34:4-10 AMPC

" Listen to my testimony: I cried to God in my distress and he answered me. He freed me from all my fears! Gaze upon him, join your life with his, and joy will come. Your faces will glisten with glory. You'll never wear that shame-face again. When I had nothing, desperate and defeated, I cried out to the Lord and he heard me, bringing his miracle-deliverance when I needed it most. The angel of the Lord stooped down to listen as I prayed, encircling me, empowering me, and showing me how to escape. He will do this for everyone who fears God. Drink deeply of the pleasures of this God. Experience for yourself the joyous mercies he gives to all who turn to hide themselves in him. Worship in awe and wonder, all you who've been made holy! For all who fear him will feast with plenty. Even the strong and the wealthy grow weak and hungry, but those who passionately pursue the Lord will never lack any good thing."
Psalms 34:4-10 TPT

The word of GOD is clear that HE is always listening. HE longs for personal interaction with us.

"The Lord sees all we do; he watches over his friends day and night. His godly ones receive the answers they seek whenever they cry out to him."
Psalms 34:15 TPT

"The eyes of the Lord are toward the [uncompromisingly] righteous and His ears are open to their cry."
Psalm 34:15 AMPC

" The eyes of the Lord are upon the righteous, and his ears are open unto their cry.'
Psalms 34:15 KJV

" The righteous cry, and the Lord heareth, and delivereth them out of all their troubles. The Lord is nigh unto them that are of a broken heart; and saveth such as be of a contrite spirit. Many are the afflictions of the righteous: but the Lord delivereth him out of them all."
Psalms 34:17-19 KJV

"When the righteous cry for help, the Lord hears, and delivers them out of all their distress and troubles. The Lord is close to those who are of a broken heart and saves such as are crushed with sorrow for sin and are humbly and thoroughly penitent. Many evils confront the [consistently] righteous, but the Lord delivers him out of them all."
Psalm 34:17-19 AMPC

"When his people pray for help, he listens and rescues them from their troubles. The Lord is there to rescue all who are discouraged and have given up hope. The Lord's people may suffer a lot, but he will always bring them safely through."
Psalms 34:17-19 CEV

The Lord watches over the righteous and listens to their cries; The righteous call to the Lord , and he listens; he rescues them from all their troubles. The Lord is near to those who are discouraged; he saves those who have lost all hope. Good people suffer many troubles, but the Lord saves them from them all;
Psalm 34:15, 17-19 GNTD

The 34th Psalm is full of the blessings that GOD gladly gives to those who love HIM. If we take the opportunity to read through the scriptures of the BIBLE we will see that our Heavenly Father is full of good plans and desires toward us. HE not only promises to be there for us in our time of need, and listen for our call. HE also, has a well thought out plan for each of HIS children's life. HIS plans are available for our benefit if we choose to follow those plans.

" I alone know the plans I have for you, plans to bring you prosperity and not disaster, plans to bring about the future you hope for. Then you will call to me. You will come and pray to me, and I will answer you. You will seek me, and you will find me because you will seek me with all your heart."
Jeremiah 29:11-13 GNTD

"For I know the thoughts and plans that I have for you, says the Lord, thoughts and plans for welfare and peace and not for evil, to give you hope in your final outcome. Then you will call upon Me, and you will come and pray to Me, and I will hear and heed you. Then you will seek Me, inquire for, and require Me [as a vital necessity] and find Me when you search for Me with all your heart. [Deut. 4:29-30.]"
Jeremiah 29:11-13 AMPC

" For I know the thoughts that I think toward you, saith the Lord , thoughts of peace, and not of evil, to give you an expected end. Then shall ye call upon me, and ye shall go and pray unto me, and I

will hearken unto you. And ye shall seek me, and find me, when ye shall search for me with all your heart."
Jeremiah 29:11-13 KJV

I encourage everyone to take advantage of the opportunity to enter into the presence of GOD boldly. Enter without fear of rejection, and make your request. HE will answer, and HE has a plan for your good.

Chapter 3

PRAYER of THANKSGIVING

"Be careful for nothing; but in every thing by prayer and supplication with thanksgiving let your requests be made known unto God."
Philippians 4:6 KJV

"Don't be pulled in different directions or worried about a thing. Be saturated in prayer throughout each day, offering your faith-filled requests before God with overflowing gratitude. Tell him every detail of your life,"
Philippians 4:6 TPT

"Do not fret or have any anxiety about anything, but in every circumstance and in everything, by prayer and petition (definite requests), with thanksgiving, continue to make your wants known to God."
Philippians 4:6 AMPC

"Do not worry about anything. Instead, pray to God about everything. Ask him to help you with the things that you need. And thank him for his help."
Philippians 4:6 EASY

"Don't worry about anything; instead, pray about everything. Tell God what you need, and thank him for all he has done."
Philippians 4:6 NLT

"Continue in prayer, and watch in the same with thanksgiving;"
Colossians 4:2 KJV

"Devote yourselves to prayer with an alert mind and a thankful heart."
Colossians 4:2 NLT

"Be earnest and unwearied and steadfast in your prayer [life], being [both] alert and intent in [your praying] with thanksgiving."
Colossians 4:2 AMPC

"Be faithful to pray as intercessors who are fully alert and giving thanks to God ."
Colossians 4:2 TPT

"Continue to pray seriously. Stay awake, like people who watch carefully. And remember to thank God."
Colossians 4:2 EASY

"Now when Daniel knew that the writing was signed, he went into his house; and his windows being open in his chamber toward Jerusalem, he kneeled upon his knees three times a day, and prayed, and gave thanks before his God, as he did aforetime."
Daniel 6:10 KJV

"Then on that day David delivered first this psalm to thank the Lord into the hand of Asaph and his brethren. Give thanks unto the Lord , call upon his name, make known his deeds among the people. Seek the Lord and his strength, seek his face continually."
1 Chronicles 16:7-8, 11 KJV

"Then on that day David first entrusted to Asaph and his brethren the singing of thanks to the Lord [as their chief task]: O give thanks to the Lord, call on His name; make known His doings among the peoples! Seek the Lord and His strength; yearn for and seek His face and to be in His presence continually!"
1 Chronicles 16:7-8, 11 AMPC

"On that day David gave to Asaph and his fellow Levites this song of thanksgiving to the Lord : Give thanks to the Lord and proclaim his greatness. Let the whole world know what he has done. Search for the Lord and for his strength; continually seek him."
1 Chronicles 16:7-8, 11 NLT

"On that day, David first told Asaph and the other Levites that they should thank the Lord with this song. Give thanks to the Lord . Shout to him. Tell the people among the nations what he has done. Look towards the Lord ! Because he is strong, ask him to help you. Always try to find him."
1 Chronicles 16:7-8, 11 EASY

"And Mattaniah the son of Mica, the son of Zabdi, the son of Asaph, was the principal to begin the thanksgiving in prayer:"
Nehemiah 11:17a KJV

"Enter into his gates with thanksgiving, and into his courts with praise: be thankful unto him, and bless his name."
Psalms 100:4 KJV

"I will offer to thee the sacrifice of thanksgiving, and will call upon the name of the Lord ."
Psalms 116:17 KJV

"And he took the seven loaves and the fishes, and gave thanks, and brake them, and gave to his disciples, and the disciples to the multitude."
Matthew 15:36; Mark 8.6; John 6.11 KJV

"Wherefore I also, after I heard of your faith in the Lord Jesus, and love unto all the saints, Cease not to give thanks for you, making mention of you in my prayers;"
Ephesians 1:15-16 KJV

"We give thanks to God always for you all, making mention of you in our prayers;"
1 Thessalonians 1:2 KJV

"Pray without ceasing. In everything give thanks: for this is the will of God in Christ Jesus concerning you."
1 Thessalonians 5:17-18 KJV

"I exhort therefore, that, first of all, supplications, prayers, intercessions, and giving of thanks, be made for all men;"
1 Timothy 2:1 KJV

There are so many scriptures in the Bible which teach us how important it is to offer prayers of Thanksgiving. The act of saying thank you to GOD is a practiced form of communication which expresses our sincere gratitude to The FATHER, acknowledging His great and wonderful activity in our lives. Somebody said, "If You woke up today, and had only what you thanked God for yesterday, how much would you have?" We have a great shortcoming in our lives when it comes to showing our gratitude toward GOD. We have a tendency to take things for granted, often until we encounter situations which cause us to stop and take stock of the value of something or someone from which or whom we have been separated.

I have often wondered about our social norms and the courtesies which many of us were taught to observe in school and in our homes when we were young. Prominent in that list, is the practice of saying Thank you when we want to show our appreciation. I have found it impossible for me to pray, and to go throughout my day without thank you coming out of my mouth often. When I discovered the principle of Matthew 12.34b, "...for out of the abundance of the heart the mouth speaketh." Thank you can only come out of my mouth if thank you is in my heart. Excuse me, but I am happy for the things that come out of my mouth, they serve as a constant reminder of what I have allowed to enter into my soul. Every thank you is another form of communication between me and GOD. I believe that we are living a life of constant prayer in every moment. Thinking about the words we say as an act of communication between ourselves and our Heavenly Father. Wow, even the activity of putting these thoughts together causes me to be filled with thanks to GOD, WHO has invested HIMSELF in my heart and given me a chance to express my gratitude here in this book. Thank you LORD!

I pray that we purposely put in the effort to become more thankful in our communication with GOD. After all, it just seems rude to always make prayers of petition and never offer prayers of Thanksgiving. I believe that GOD smiles when HIS children say Thank you. Who else could do these things but GOD? As a father and a grandfather, it makes me smile to hear the words Thank you from my children and grandchildren. How much more wonderful, and powerful it is in the spirit realm, when we lift our voices in thanks unto GOD, silencing the attempts of the enemy to bring us into a place of complacency and ingratitude. So, the next time you find yourself preparing to make a petition before GOD, remember:

"Don't be pulled in different directions or worried about a thing. Be saturated in prayer throughout each day, offering your faith-filled requests before God with overflowing gratitude. Tell him every detail of your life,"
Philippians 4:6 TPT

When I was growing up, there would frequently be "Altar, or Tarrying Services." During these times of the service those who were responsible for working the Altar, would encourage all of those who would be kneeling at the Altar as supplicants to cry out to The LORD in different ways. I wonder, when the saints in the church used to tell those who would be kneeling at the altar, "Tell Him Thank ya!" I wonder if they really knew what they were saying.

Chapter 4

Prayer of Agreement

"Again I say unto you, That if two of you shall agree on earth as touching any thing that they shall ask, it shall be done for them of my Father which is in heaven."
Matthew 18:19 KJV

"Again I tell you, if two of you on earth agree (harmonize together, make a symphony together) about whatever [anything and everything] they may ask, it will come to pass and be done for them by My Father in heaven."
Matthew 18:19 AMPC

"I promise that when any two of you on earth agree about something you are praying for, my Father in heaven will do it for you."
Matthew 18:19 CEV

"Two people may agree together to ask God for something. If they agree like that, then my Father in heaven will give them what they ask for."
Matthew 18:19 EASY

"Again, I give you an eternal truth: If two of you agree to ask God for something in a symphony of prayer, my heavenly Father will do it for you."
Matthew 18:19 TPT

What makes this form of prayer so powerful to me is that Jesus encourages the unified prayer between two believers. What naturally follows, and what I teach Married Couples, is the power of agreement in marriage, coming together and developing a mindset of unity or one flesh in their prayer lives. By doing this, a married couple is able to tap into another source of strength available to them as well. That is the power of Covenant. The covenant bond provided to believers through marriage is designed to resemble the covenant bond that the FATHER GOD has entered into with believers through the Lord JESUS. It's encouraging enough to know that GOD answers the prayers of even one of HIS children. How exciting is it to know that HE extends a promise which can only increase and strengthen the bond between two covenant believers. Knowing that a marriage bond can only be enlarged by agreement is empowering. This should provide real incentive for a man and a woman to ensure that they have no unsettled issues which could possibly disrupt their agreement. This reality promotes focus on the things which are truly important

What is also powerful is the way the Amplified Bible puts it, **"...*harmonize, together, make a symphony together...*"** I have always been intrigued by the power of harmonizing. Harmonizing takes sounds that are, clearly distinct and individual in themselves, but can come together to create a fuller sound that fits perfectly, thereby creating something pleasing to the ears of the listener. Then there's the symphony, which requires a conductor's authority in order to operate properly. It speaks to me of two believers who have sought the mind and heart of GOD before praying. It enables the believers to pray more effectively, because they have come together in a covenant of agreement to pray what they believe is the will of GOD concerning a situation. This indicates that praying a prayer of agreement is not just two people deciding that they want something, and then going to GOD and asking for it in order to selfishly receive. If that was the case, then two people could just take turns every other day asking GOD for each other's desires, and expecting to receive. Clearly this form of prayer requires a measure of selflessness by each individual, as they humbly agree on the will of GOD in a situation, and then go boldly before HIS throne of grace fully expecting to receive the thing for which they have prayed. HALLELUJAH!!! So, when I pray this type of prayer, because I believe GOD's word is magnificently powerful, I will combine this with 1 John 5.14, 15:

" Also, we can really trust God to help us when we turn to him. We know that he will hear us. When we ask for anything that he wants us to have, he listens to us. Since we know that, we also know that God will give to us the things that we ask for. It is like we have already received those things from him."
1 John 5:14-15 EASY

It strengthens my resolve and encourages me when I also read Ecclesiastes 4.9:

"Two are better than one; because they have a good reward for their labour. For if they fall, the one will lift up his fellow: but woe to him that is alone when he falleth; for he hath not another to help him up. Again, if two lie together, then they have heat: but how can one be warm alone? And if one prevail against him, two shall withstand him; and a threefold cord is not quickly broken."
Ecclesiastes 4:9-12 KJV

"Two people are better off than one, for they can help each other succeed. If one person falls, the other can reach out and help. But someone who falls alone is in real trouble. Likewise, two people lying close together can keep each other warm. But how can one be warm alone? A person standing alone can be attacked and defeated, but two can stand back-to-back and conquer. Three are even better, for a triple-braided cord is not easily broken."

Ecclesiastes 4:9-12 NLT

"We" is always more effective than "I" when there are two people willing to come together and join their faith in petitioning GOD. The strength provided when each participant gives support to the other during the process. The enemy is much less likely to break up the plan when each is supportive of the other. Then when the Presence of GOD is included, the three cords together are even stronger than two.

But the principle doesn't end there. The scripture indicates that more than two people can agree when they pray. There is an understanding in the language that agreement in prayer is more powerful when even more people choose to come together in a unified prayer to petition GOD for a resolution, for HIS involvement, for an impartation in or for a specific situation. This is why corporate prayer times can be so powerful. Congregational prayer times, prayer groups, or prayer meetings can be game changers in the process of implementing the plan of GOD. I have seen, and expect to see even more in the future, supernatural activity manifest even more frequently as GOD'S people come together crying out in faith and expectation of the guaranteed manifestation of the change which is being requested. HALLELUJA!!! If you are an Ecclesiastical Leader, and you don't have or belong to a prayer group in your ministry; what are you waiting for? If you are a believer you should be an active partner in a local ministry, and you should be a part of a prayer group in that ministry actively petitioning the presence of GOD in unity fully expecting HIM to respond to your prayers.

So, many people say they believe in GOD, but struggle to believe what HIS word says concerning prayer. How can we have faith that HE will save us, but then struggle to believe that HE not only wants to, but will heal us, or provide another need in our lives? The same faith that causes us to receive salvation, by believing that JESUS, the only begotten Son of GOD, shed HIS blood and died to pay the price of our redemption, that same faith is strong enough to work for anyone who wants to pray for GOD to meet the other needs in their life. Believe and Agree, Pray and Receive, In JESUS' Name!!!

Chapter 5

Prayer of Repentance

"If my people, which are called by my name, shall humble themselves, and pray, and seek my face, and turn from their wicked ways; then will I hear from heaven, and will forgive their sin, and will heal their land." 2 Chronicles 7.14kjv

"Now mine eyes shall be open, and mine ears attent unto the prayer that is made in this place. For now have I chosen and sanctified this house, that my name may be there forever: and mine eyes and mine heart shall be there perpetually"   2 Chronicles 7.15,16kjv

"Yet have thou respect unto the prayer of thy servant, and to his supplication, O Lord my God, to hearken unto the cry and to the prayer, which thy servant prayeth before thee to day: That thine eyes may be open toward this house night and day, even toward the place of which thou hast said, My name shall be there: that thou mayest hearken unto the prayer which thy servant shall make toward this place. And hearken thou to the supplication of thy servant, and of thy people Israel, when they shall pray toward this place: and hear thou in heaven thy dwelling place: and when thou hearest, forgive. If any man trespass against his neighbour, and an oath be laid upon him to cause him to swear, and the oath come before thine altar in this house: Then hear thou in heaven, and do, and judge thy servants, condemning the wicked, to bring his way upon his head; and justifying the righteous, to give him according to his righteousness. When thy people Israel be smitten down before the enemy, because they have sinned against thee, and shall turn again to thee, and confess thy name, and pray, and make supplication unto thee in this house: Then hear thou in heaven, and forgive the sin of thy people Israel, and bring them again unto the land which thou gavest unto their fathers. When heaven is shut up, and there is no rain, because they have sinned against thee; if they pray toward this place, and confess thy name, and turn from their sin, when thou afflictest them: Then hear thou in heaven, and forgive the sin of thy servants, and of thy people Israel, that thou teach them the good way wherein they should walk, and give rain upon thy land, which thou hast given to thy people for an inheritance. If there be in the land famine, if there be pestilence, blasting, mildew, locust, or if there be caterpiller; if their enemy besiege them in the land of their cities; whatsoever plague, whatsoever sickness there be; What prayer and supplication soever be made by any man, or by all thy people Israel, which shall know every man the plague of his own heart, and spread forth his hands toward this house: Then hear thou in heaven thy dwelling place, and forgive, and do, and give to every man according to his ways, whose heart thou knowest; (for thou, even thou only, knowest the hearts of all the children of men;) That they may fear thee all the days that they live in the land which thou gavest unto our fathers. Moreover concerning a stranger, that is not of thy people Israel, but cometh out of a far country for thy name's sake; (For they shall hear of thy great name, and of thy strong hand, and of thy stretched out arm;) when he shall come and pray toward this house; Hear thou in heaven thy dwelling place, and do according to all that the stranger calleth to thee for: that all people of the earth may know thy name, to fear thee, as do thy people Israel; and that they may know that this house, which I have builded, is called by thy name. If thy people go out to battle against their enemy, whithersoever thou shalt send them, and shall pray unto the Lord toward the city which thou hast chosen, and toward the house that I have built for thy name: Then hear thou in heaven their prayer and their supplication, and maintain their cause. If they sin against thee, (for there is no man that sinneth not,) and thou be angry with them, and deliver them to the enemy, so that they carry them away captives unto the land of the enemy, far or near; Yet if they shall bethink themselves in the land whither they were carried captives, and repent, and make supplication unto thee in the land of them that carried them captives, saying, We have sinned, and have done perversely, we have committed wickedness; And so return unto thee with all their heart, and with all their soul, in the land of their enemies, which led them away captive, and pray unto thee toward their land, which thou gavest unto their fathers, the city which thou hast chosen, and the house which I have built for thy name: Then hear thou their prayer and their supplication in heaven thy dwelling place, and maintain their cause, And forgive thy people that have sinned against thee, and all their transgressions wherein they have transgressed against thee, and give them compassion before them who carried them captive, that they may have compassion on

them: For they be thy people, and thine inheritance, which thou broughtest forth out of Egypt, from the midst of the furnace of iron: That thine eyes may be open unto the supplication of thy servant, and unto the supplication of thy people Israel, to hearken unto them in all that they call for unto thee. For thou didst separate them from among all the people of the earth, to be thine inheritance, as thou spakest by the hand of Moses thy servant, when thou broughtest our fathers out of Egypt, O Lord God . And it was so, that when Solomon had made an end of praying all this prayer and supplication unto the Lord , he arose from before the altar of the Lord , from kneeling on his knees with his hands spread up to heaven."
1 Kings 8:28-54 KJV

"I say unto you, that likewise joy shall be in heaven over one sinner that repenteth, more than over ninety and nine just persons, which need no repentance." Luke 15.7kjv

"Take heed to yourselves: If thy brother trespass against thee, rebuke him; and if he repent, forgive him. And if he trespass against thee seven times in a day, and seven times in a day turn again to thee, saying, I repent; thou shalt forgive him." Luke 17.3,4kjv

"Be alert. If you see your friend going wrong, correct him. If he responds, forgive him. Even if it's personal against you and repeated seven times through the day, and seven times he says, ' I'm sorry, I won't do it again,' forgive him."   Luke 17.3,4 MSG

"And the times of this ignorance God winked at; but now commandeth all men everywhere to repent;" Acts 17.30kjv

"In those days John the Baptist came to the Judean wilderness and began preaching. His message was, "Repent of your sins and turn to God, for the Kingdom of Heaven is near. " The prophet Isaiah was speaking about John when he said, "He is a voice shouting in the wilderness, 'Prepare the way for the Lord 's coming! Clear the road for him!'" People from Jerusalem and from all of Judea and all over the Jordan Valley went out to see and hear John. And when they confessed their sins, he baptized them in the Jordan River. But when he saw many Pharisees and Sadducees coming to watch him baptize, he denounced them. "You brood of snakes!" he exclaimed. "Who warned you to flee the coming wrath? Prove by the way you

live that you have repented of your sins and turned to God."
Matthew 3:1-3, 5-8 NLT

"Testifying both to the Jews, and also to the Greeks, repentance toward God, and faith toward our Lord Jesus Christ".
Acts 20:21 KJV

"Therefore thou art inexcusable, O man, whosoever thou art that judgest: for wherein thou judgest another, thou condemnest thyself; for thou that judgest doest the same things. But we are sure that the judgment of God is according to truth against them which commit such things. And thinkest thou this, O man, that judgest them which do such things, and doest the same, that thou shalt escape the judgment of God? Or despisest thou the riches of his goodness and forbearance and longsuffering; not knowing that the goodness of God leadeth thee to repentance?"
Romans 2:1-4 KJV

"For godly sorrow worketh repentance to salvation not to be repented of: but the sorrow of the world worketh death".
2 Corinthians 7:10 KJV

"Therefore leaving the principles of the doctrine of Christ, let us go on unto perfection; not laying again the foundation of repentance from dead works, and of faith toward God, Of the doctrine of baptisms, and of laying on of hands, and of resurrection of the dead, and of eternal judgment."
Hebrews 6:1-2 KJV

"The Lord is not slack concerning his promise, as some men count slackness; but is longsuffering to us-ward, not willing that any should perish, but that all should come to repentance".
2 Peter 3:9 KJV

The significance of this type of prayer goes way beyond what we read. When I give consideration to this, I am strengthened to see the work of GOD'S mercy in forgiveness, which goes beyond repentance. One of the greatest elements of our salvation relationship with GOD through JESUS CHRIST is our personal confession. It's not just about whether or not GOD will forgive us, but it is more important for us to know, that HE already has forgiven us. It is the actual confession from our mouth, which is representative of the faith within our hearts that causes the active release of GOD'S grace of forgiveness upon us. Remember we can only confess a truth which is already established in our heart. So then, Repentance, Forgiveness, and Salvation which were previously completed through the life, death, burial, and resurrection of JESUS, are all released upon our lives through the confession, or more specifically our own words of Faith.

If Prayer is a personal conversation between any person and GOD, then the confession of my lips which activates the promises of GOD becomes a time of prayer received and responded to by GOD.

"If we confess our sins, he is faithful and just to forgive us our sins, and to cleanse us from all unrighteousness".
1 John 1:9 KJV

"But what saith it? The word is nigh thee, even in thy mouth, and in thy heart: that is, the word of faith, which we preach; That if thou shalt confess with thy mouth the Lord Jesus, and shalt believe in thine heart that God hath raised him from the dead, thou shalt be saved. For with the heart man believeth unto righteousness; and with the mouth confession is made unto salvation."
Romans 10:8-10 KJV

I choose to maintain a constant expectation of The FATHER, and HIS unchanging character. I believe that HE is attentive to me, and to every word I speak. HE remains ready to respond to the voice of my heart.

"And it shall come to pass, that before they call, I will answer; and while they are yet speaking, I will hear."
Isaiah 65:24 KJV

"I will answer them before they even call to me. While they are still talking about their needs, I will go ahead and answer their prayers!"
Isaiah 65:24 NLT

What an incredible opportunity to be in a relationship with the Almighty GOD. Because I am intimately acquainted with HIM, I can depend upon HIM to be attentive to my voice and fully ready to fulfill my request. Not only that, but HE offers to reveal hidden secrets to those who ask.

"Thus saith the Lord the maker thereof, the Lord that formed it, to establish it; the Lord is his name; Call unto me, and I will answer thee, and shew thee great and mighty things, which thou knowest not".
Jeremiah 33:2-3 KJV

Chapter 6

Worship and Praise the Sounds of Prayer

The Power of the Tongue is a familiar theme of ministry today. However this is most often used as a way of encouraging believers to be mindful of your words, and the need to speak positively. However, in this chapter I want to enlarge upon a revelation which has become increasingly clear.

"A time will come, however, indeed it is already here, when the true (genuine) worshipers will worship the Father in spirit and in truth (reality); for the Father is seeking just such people as these as His worshipers. God is a Spirit (a spiritual Being) and those who worship Him must worship Him in spirit and in truth (reality)."
John 4:23-24 AMPC

"But the hour cometh, and now is, when the true worshippers shall worship the Father in spirit and in truth: for the Father seeketh such to worship him. God is a Spirit: and they that worship him must worship him in spirit and in truth."
John 4:23-24 KJV

"But the time is coming—indeed it's here now—when true worshipers will worship the Father in spirit and in truth. The Father is looking for those who will worship him that way. For God is Spirit, so those who worship him must worship in spirit and in truth."
John 4:23-24 NLT

So, is our Worship a time of Prayer? Should we be conscious of how our worship goes over in the Heavenly realm? If we determine that prayer is a personal opportunity for intimate communication between ourselves and GOD, then anytime we open communication we can consider it prayer. GOD clearly responds to our praise, and our worship.

" But thou art holy, O thou that inhabitest the praises of Israel."
Psalms 22:3 KJV

"But You are holy, O You Who dwell in [the holy place where] the praises of Israel [are offered]. Our fathers trusted in You; they trusted (leaned on, relied on You, and were confident) and You delivered them. They cried to You and were delivered; they trusted in, leaned on, and confidently relied on You, and were not ashamed or confounded or disappointed."
Psalm 22:3-5 AMPC

As I read these scriptures, I see that GOD shows up, HE responds to the praise of HIS people. The Amplified version of the Bible, in Psalms 22, shows that the praise of GOD during prayer brings GOD's presence into our situation. When we long to touch GOD's presence in prayer, we will find that HE is available when we combine praise with prayer. We can find similar results when we examine the effect of worship in the scripture.

"Then Jesus went thence, and departed into the coasts of Tyre and Sidon. And, behold, a woman of Canaan came out of the same coasts, and cried unto him, saying, Have mercy on me, O Lord, thou Son of David; my daughter is grievously vexed with a devil. But he answered her not a word. And his disciples came and besought him, saying, Send her away; for she crieth after us. But he answered and said, I am not sent but unto the lost sheep of the house of Israel. Then came she and worshipped him, saying, Lord, help me. But he answered and said, It is not meet to take the children's bread, and to cast it to dogs. And she said, Truth, Lord:

yet the dogs eat of the crumbs which fall from their masters' table. Then Jesus answered and said unto her, O woman, great is thy faith: be it unto thee even as thou wilt. And her daughter was made whole from that very hour."
Matthew 15:21-28 KJV

I have found that my worship time and my prayer time are always one and the same. When we understand that worship is more than a particular song, rather it is the sound of our heart connecting with the sound of HIS heart. It is that connection which releases the power of HIS presence. HIS presence is the place where we get what we need and desire from GOD.

"Thou wilt shew me the path of life: in thy presence is fulness of joy; at thy right hand there are pleasures for evermore."
Psalms 16:11 KJV

The ultimate purpose of my prayer time is to have personal fellowship with The FATHER. There is no place like HIS presence. I delight in spending personal time with HIM. There is nothing that compares to that joy filled experience. It is an experience which also comes with benefits.

"The young lions do lack, and suffer hunger: but they that seek the Lord shall not want any good thing."
Psalms 34:10 KJV

"Delight thyself also in the Lord ; and he shall give thee the desires of thine heart."
Psalms 37:4 KJV

"Delight yourself also in the Lord, and He will give you the desires and secret petitions of your heart."
Psalm 37:4 AMPC

"Enjoy serving the Lord , and he will give you what you want."
Psalms 37:4 NCV

Benefits are a part of the promise of GOD to HIS children. When I praise or worship GOD, I never enter into the activity with any thought of benefits. However, HE chooses to make the benefits available to me as an example of HIS overflowing love for those who demonstrate their love for HIM.

When you begin to consider the prayer of thanksgiving, it is not difficult to realize how closely related these types of prayer actually are. So, once again moving beyond a paradigm, which limits the definition of prayer to only a specific time set aside for nothing else. I truly believe that the words of our mouth which are inspired by and proceed from our relationship with GOD must be considered a time of communication with GOD. It just makes sense to believe that our GOD Who places so much emphasis on the life giving power contained within every word we speak, would embrace the communication which proceedeth forth from our mouth, a form of prayer, as long as that communication is directed toward HIM. Every form of our Spirit inspired communication with HIM is a form of prayer.

Finally, we need to understand that Jude encourages us to increase the impact of our times of fellowship with GOD by combining praise and worship with prayer as we enter into the realm of The Spirit of GOD. Jude wants to communicate to us that by combining these elements, our prayer is empowered beyond the opposition of the enemy as we enter in and release the agents of Heaven to operate on our behalf.

"Let the word of Christ dwell in you richly in all wisdom; teaching and admonishing one another in psalms and hymns and spiritual songs, singing with grace in your hearts to the Lord."
Colossians 3:16 KJV

" Speaking to yourselves in psalms and hymns and spiritual songs, singing and making melody in your heart to the Lord;"
Ephesians 5:19 KJV

But you, beloved, build yourselves up [founded] on your most holy faith [make progress, rise like an edifice higher and higher], praying in the Holy Spirit;
Jude 1:20 AMPC

Never underestimate the sounds that attract GOD'S attention. David never underestimated the value of praise and worship. In fact, he said that it was so valuable to him that he was wholly committed to it. He saw praise and worship as an essential part of his existence.

"I will bless the Lord at all times: his praise shall continually be in my mouth."
Psalms 34:1 KJV

"I will praise the Lord at all times. I will constantly speak his praises."
Psalms 34:1 NLT

"I bless God every chance I get; my lungs expand with his praise."
Psalm 34:1 MSG

If we wanted to see what a powerful prayer life produces, we would find revelation in the life and ministry of the Apostle Paul. No one was able to demonstrate the multiple forms of prayer and then articulate them more excellently than Paul. There are examples of every form of prayer which is included in this book written about within the letters of Paul. So it is that we are able to see that Praise and Worship is integral to our relationship with GOD.

"Speaking to yourselves in psalms and hymns and spiritual songs, singing and making melody in your heart to the Lord;"
Ephesians 5:19 KJV

"Speak out to one another in psalms and hymns and spiritual songs, offering praise with voices [and instruments] and making melody with all your heart to the Lord,"
Ephesians 5:19 AMPC

"Don't drink too much wine. That cheapens your life. Drink the Spirit of God, huge draughts of him. Sing hymns instead of drinking songs! Sing songs from your heart to Christ. Sing praises over everything, any excuse for a song to God the Father in the name of our Master, Jesus Christ."
Ephesians 5:18-20 MSG

Let Praise arise when we pray so miracles can happen suddenly!

"And when they had laid many stripes upon them, they cast them into prison, charging the jailor to keep them safely: Who, having received such a charge, thrust them into the inner prison, and made their feet fast in the stocks. And at midnight Paul and Silas prayed, and sang praises unto God: and the prisoners heard them. And suddenly there was a great earthquake, so that the foundations of the prison were shaken: and immediately all the doors were opened, and every one's bands were loosed."
Acts 16:23-26 KJV

"When her owners saw that their lucrative little business was suddenly bankrupt, they went after Paul and Silas, roughed them up and dragged them into the market square. Then the police arrested

them and pulled them into a court with the accusation, "These men are disturbing the peace—dangerous Jewish agitators subverting our Roman law and order." By this time the crowd had turned into a restless mob out for blood. The judges went along with the mob, had Paul and Silas's clothes ripped off and ordered a public beating. After beating them black-and-blue, they threw them into jail, telling the jailkeeper to put them under heavy guard so there would be no chance of escape. He did just that—threw them into the maximum security cell in the jail and clamped leg irons on them. Along about midnight, Paul and Silas were at prayer and singing a robust hymn to God. The other prisoners couldn't believe their ears. Then, without warning, a huge earthquake! The jailhouse tottered, every door flew open, all the prisoners were loose".
Acts 16:22-26 MSG

"And when they had struck them with many blows, they threw them into prison, charging the jailer to keep them safely. He, having received [so strict a] charge, put them into the inner prison (the dungeon) and fastened their feet in the stocks. But about midnight, as Paul and Silas were praying and singing hymns of praise to God, and the [other] prisoners were listening to them, Suddenly there was a great earthquake, so that the very foundations of the prison were shaken; and at once all the doors were opened and everyone's shackles were unfastened."
Acts 16:23-26 AMPC

I Praise and Worship and I pray all at once. Power is in HIS presence, and HE certainly responds to the sounds each of those forms of prayer produce. Let YOUR name(JEHOVAH) be exalted by my voice, I need YOUR presence where I am. In this moment, and in this place!!!

Chapter 7

Praying the Word of GOD

"For ever, O Lord , thy word is settled in heaven."
Psalms 119:89 KJV

"Forever, O Lord, Your word is settled in heaven [stands firm as the heavens]."   [Ps. 89:2; Matt. 24:34, 35; I Pet. 1:25.]
Psalm 119:89 AMPC

"I will worship toward thy holy temple, and praise thy name for thy lovingkindness and for thy truth: for thou hast magnified thy word above all thy name."
Psalms 138:2 KJV

"I will worship toward Your holy temple and praise Your name for Your loving-kindness and for Your truth and faithfulness; for You have exalted above all else Your name and Your word and You have magnified Your word above all Your name!"
Psalm 138:2 AMPC

Years ago HOLY SPIRIT gave me this revelation: "Your Mouth releasing the Word of GOD in faith is the most powerful force in the earth realm. Every other activity of your life responds to this power."

Find a promise in the word of GOD and pray it. Find a scripture, and give it back to GOD. HE delights to hear HIS word, and to see it become real in HIS children's lives. It is HIS desire to do it, to make what seems intangible, tangible. A very real principle in teaching people the potential and power of this way of praying is to get believers to, "Pray the Promises and the Principles of the Word of GOD, and not the problems which we face." One of the most exciting aspects of my prayer life is the opportunity to put the power of GOD on display. Remember that throughout the Bible we see instances of manifested results after GOD speaks or after HIS word is spoken.

"For as the rain cometh down, and the snow from heaven, and returneth not thither, but watereth the earth, and maketh it bring forth and bud, that it may give seed to the sower, and bread to the eater: So shall my word be that goeth forth out of my mouth: it shall not return unto me void, but it shall accomplish that which I please, and it shall prosper in the thing whereto I sent it."
Isaiah 55:10-11 KJV

"The rain and snow come down from the heavens and stay on the ground to water the earth. They cause the grain to grow, producing seed for the farmer and bread for the hungry. It is the same with my word. I send it out, and it always produces fruit. It will accomplish all I want it to, and it will prosper everywhere I send it."
Isaiah 55:10-11 NLT

When I pray the word of GOD, I am primarily doing two things: first, I am reminding HIM of what HE said to HIS children to build up their faith in HIM.

"So then faith cometh by hearing, and hearing by the word of God." Romans 10.17 KJV

"**Faith**, then, is birthed in a heart that responds to God's anointed utterance of the Anointed One."
Romans 10:17 TPT

"So faith comes by hearing [what is told], and what is heard comes by the preaching [of the message that came from the lips] of Christ (the Messiah Himself)."
Romans 10:17 AMPC

"So faith comes from hearing the Good News, and people hear the Good News when someone tells them about Christ."
Romans 10:17 NCV

Then, after I have exercised my faith in HIM, by reminding HIM of HIS word; the second thing I do is, I give HIM the opportunity to prove HIMSELF by upholding HIS word in my life. HE always keeps HIS promises. (Hallelujah!)

"For all the promises of God in him are yea, and in him Amen, unto the glory of God by us."
2 Corinthians 1:20 KJV

"For all of God's promises find their "yes" of fulfillment in him. And as his "yes" and our "amen" ascend to God, we bring him glory!"
2 Corinthians 1:20 TPT

"For all of God's promises have been fulfilled in Christ with a resounding "Yes!" And through Christ, our "Amen" (which means "Yes") ascends to God for his glory."
2 Corinthians 1:20 NLT

"For as many as are the promises of God, they all find their Yes [answer] in Him [Christ]. For this reason we also utter the Amen (so be it) to God through Him [in His Person and by His agency] to the glory of God."
2 Corinthians 1:20 AMPC

When you don't have a prayer plan, or a prayer-point outline, just begin to use your prayer time as a time of confessing HIS word. This is an active part of my prayer time. Psalms, Proverbs, and the letters of Paul are a great source of scriptures to use in your arsenal of prayer. Put HIM in remembrance of HIS word.

"Then said the LORD unto me, Thou hast well seen: for I will hasten my word to perform it."
Jeremiah 1:12 KJV —

"Then said the LORD to me, You have well seen: for I watch over my word to perform it."
Jeremiah 1:12 HNV —

"I have set watchmen upon your walls, O Jerusalem, who will never hold their peace day or night; you who [are His servants and by your prayers] put the Lord in remembrance [of His promises], keep not silence,"
Isaiah 62:6 AMPC

"For I am the Lord : I will speak, and the word that I shall speak shall come to pass; it shall be no more prolonged: for in your days, O rebellious house, will I say the word, and will perform it, saith the Lord God ."
Ezekiel 12:25 KJV

"For I am the Lord; I will speak, and the word that I shall speak shall be performed (come to pass); it shall be no more delayed or prolonged, for in your days, O rebellious house, I will speak the word and will perform it, says the Lord God."
Ezekiel 12:25 AMPC

"Therefore say unto them, Thus saith the Lord God ; There shall none of my words be prolonged any more, but the word which I have spoken shall be done, saith the Lord God ."
Ezekiel 12:28 KJV

"Therefore say to them, Thus says the Lord God: There shall none of My words be deferred any more, but the word which I have spoken shall be performed, says the Lord God."
Ezekiel 12:28 AMPC

"So the king hearkened not unto the people: for the cause was of God, that the Lord might perform his word, which he spake by the hand of Ahijah the Shilonite to Jeroboam the son of Nebat."

2 Chronicles 10:15 KJV

"Bless the Lord , ye his angels, that excel in strength, that do his commandments, hearkening unto the voice of his word."
Psalms 103:20 KJV

It is clear through these scriptures, that GOD not only wants us to remind HIM of what HE said, HE also wants us to know, that HE will stand by what HE said. HIS divine and eternal authority will back it up! Our goal should be to properly exegete The Holy Bible, (The Word,) find out what GOD said about our situation, and then pray those scriptures. Believing when we pray that there will be a definite response to our prayer.

"Therefore I say unto you, What things soever ye desire, when ye pray, believe that ye receive them, and ye shall have them."
Mark 11:24 KJV

"I tell you, you can pray for anything, and if you believe that you've received it, it will be yours."
Mark 11:24 NLT

" For this reason I am telling you, whatever you ask for in prayer, believe (trust and be confident) that it is granted to you, and you will [get it]."
Mark 11:24 AMPC

Always keep in mind that when you pray the word of GOD, that the prayers only need to be requests, or petition prayers, the first time you pray it. After that, anytime you pray the word of GOD, know that it is already done! So, those types of prayers should be used as thanksgiving. For example, you may make a request for GOD to manifest healing in your life according to 1Peter 2.24. So the next time you go to GOD with healing on your mind. You should realize that it was done the first time you made your request. So, this time when you pray you can just thank HIM for healing you according to 1Peter 2.24. Now you are praying the word of GOD as a prayer of Thanksgiving instead of another prayer of Petition. The word of GOD is a completed act, a done deal. Once GOD released it, it was settled. So once you pray it, it is also done.

"Forever, O Lord , thy word is settled in heaven."
Psalms 119:89 KJV

"What you say goes, God , and stays , as permanent as the heavens. Your truth never goes out of fashion; it's as up-to-date as the earth when the sun comes up. Your Word and truth are dependable as ever; that's what you ordered…"
Psalm 119:89 MSG

So, we don't pray the word wondering about the outcome of our prayers. We pray the word to remind GOD of our expectations, and to thank HIM in advance for seeing the reality of that faith in our lives. Praying the word of GOD provides us with a script of faith ready to have an intimate conversation and fellowship time with HIM. Just make sure that you mix in plenty of praise and worship while you fellowship with The FATHER. That way you spend more time blessing HIM than you do asking for things for yourself.

Chapter 8

Praying In Tongues

(Praying in the Holy Ghost aka Praying in The Spirit)

Praying in The Spirit requires an initial understanding of the ability to manifest a "Heavenly Language," otherwise known as the gift of speaking in other tongues. The Greek word for this is "glossolalia." The term is used as a way of describing the linguistic utterances which are a sign of the overflowing indwelling of the Person of HOLY SPIRIT. HOLY SPIRIT comes and takes up residence within our regenerated,(born again) human spirit, and leads us from within as we establish an intimate relationship with The FATHER after receiving CHRIST JESUS as our Saviour and LORD.

"On the day Pentecost was being fulfilled, all the disciples were gathered in one place. Suddenly they heard the sound of a violent blast of wind rushing into the house from out of the heavenly realm. The roar of the wind was so overpowering it was all anyone could bear! Then all at once a pillar of fire appeared before their eyes. It separated into tongues of fire that engulfed each one of them. They were all filled and equipped with the Holy Spirit and were inspired to speak in tongues—empowered by the Spirit to speak in languages they had never learned!"
Acts 2:1-4 TPT

The activity of speaking in tongues is effective as a gift given to believers and operates both publicly within the congregation and privately in our times of personal prayer, praise, and worship as well.

"God has placed in the church the following: First apostles, second prophets, third teachers, then those with gifts of miracles, gifts of divine healing, gifts of revelation knowledge, gifts of leadership, and gifts of different kinds of tongues."
1 Corinthians 12:28 TPT

Shortly after midnight one morning in January of 1983, I was awakened on the floor of my father's office in Our Lord's Temple COGIC in Ithaca, NY. I was spending a week of consecration during those days, and had received my father's permission to spend the week in the church. It wasn't unusual for me to fast and pray while separating myself. Also, my parents had embraced my spiritual bent for some time, so they were used to something like that from their 22 year old son. What was unusual about this particular night was that just after I had lain down, and just before I fell asleep, I heard HOLY SPIRIT telling me to get up and begin to pray in the Spirit. As I began to pray in my heavenly language, HOLY SPIRIT clearly instructed me to begin to rebuke the spirit of death. HE spoke to me repeatedly, telling me to rebuke the spirit of death, rebuke the spirit of death. After I specifically stood on my authority in CHRIST JESUS over the spirit of death, HOLY SPIRIT told me to begin to pray in tongues again for about another 30 minutes. The next night after having completed the consecration and being back at my parents' home, I received a phone call from my younger brother. He was calling to tell me that while working the overnight shift at an Atlanta area convenience store, he and his co-worker had been robbed at gunpoint the night before. While admittedly taken aback by the news, I was extremely thankful that my brother was alive to be calling and talking with me at that moment. The next thing I thought to ask him was, "what time was it that this was happening?" When he told me the time of this experience, I realized and told him immediately that there was clearly nothing coincidental about the timing of his experience.

That brother is my younger brother Apostle Tommy Roberts, who along with his wife Pastor Lynette currently Pastors Lifepointe Christian Faith Center in the region of Iowa City, Iowa. You see Holy Spirit used the experience of 1983 to affect our lives in such a way that we have grown into adulthood allowing us to affect people all over the world through the ministry of the gospel of JESUS CHRIST. Also, more immediately, I learned very clearly in that moment how real my relationship with GOD and the presence of HOLY SPIRIT in my life actually is. HE awakened me to give me the chance to participate in HIS plan and teach me several things at the same time. First was the importance of knowing HIS voice, even though I had never personally experienced something so immediately important. The second was the necessity of complete obedience by faith when HE hadn't even told me who to pray for specifically. The next thing Holy Spirit taught me was that HE is looking for people who HE can trust to pray and impact the earth by operating in conjunction with the spirit realm to continue to implement the plan of GOD. When we pray in our heavenly language we are allowing HOLY SPIRIT to pray through us to release The FATHER'S will in the earth. As we yield our regenerated human spirit and our tongue to HIM, HE gives instructions to Angelic beings, the Hosts of Heaven to operate in the earth to implement the plans of The FATHER, and they are empowered and strengthened when we Pray in Tongues.

" Likewise the Spirit also helpeth our infirmities: for we know not what we should pray for as we ought: but the Spirit itself maketh intercession for us with groanings which cannot be uttered."
Romans 8:26 KJV

"Meanwhile, the moment we get tired in the waiting, God's Spirit is right alongside helping us along. If we don't know how or what to pray, it doesn't matter. He does our praying in and for us, making prayer out of our wordless sighs, our aching groans. He knows us far better than we know ourselves, knows our pregnant condition, and keeps us present before God. That's why we can be so sure that every detail in our lives of love for God is worked into something good."
Romans 8:26-28 MSG

"So too the [Holy] Spirit comes to our aid and bears us up in our weakness; for we do not know what prayer to offer nor how to offer it worthily as we ought, but the Spirit Himself goes to meet our supplication and pleads in our behalf with unspeakable yearnings and groanings too deep for utterance."
Romans 8:26 AMPC

"Similarly, the Spirit helps us in our weakness; for we don't know how to pray the way we should. But the Spirit himself pleads on our behalf with groanings too deep for words;"
Romans (Rom) 8:26 CJB

"in the same way, the Spirit helps us in our weakness, for we do not know how we should pray, but the Spirit himself intercedes for us with inexpressible groanings."
Romans 8:26 NET

*******"Bless the Lord , ye his angels, that excel in strength, that do his commandments, hearkening unto the voice of his word. Bless ye the Lord , all ye his hosts; ye ministers of his, that do his

pleasure."******
Psalms 103:20-21 KJV

So, not only are we allowing HOLY SPIRIT to pray through us in a Heavenly Language, but the Angels of GOD, and the Hosts of Heaven are hearkening to the voice of GOD'S word. We are the ones who give voice to the word. I get excited when I understand that the definition the of the word **hearken** means: to listen with the intent to **Do.** Also, as a matter of Spiritual revelational fact, when the former angel lucifer was cast down from his position in heaven, he lost his connection to understanding spiritual language; he does not know our spiritual intents. So, he can only respond to our revealed words and actions. Thankfully GOD has given us Angelic assistance to empower our confessions, and strengthen our prayers before Heaven.

"And there was war in heaven: Michael and his angels fought against the dragon; and the dragon fought and his angels, And prevailed not; neither was their place found any more in heaven. And the great dragon was cast out, that old serpent, called the Devil, and Satan, which deceiveth the whole world: he was cast out into the earth, and his angels were cast out with him".
Revelation 12:7-9 KJV

"And he said unto them, I beheld Satan as lightning fall from heaven."
Luke 10:18 KJV

"Jesus replied, "While you were ministering, I watched Satan topple until he fell suddenly from heaven like lightning to the ground."
Luke 10:18 TPT

When we pray In The SPIRIT, In The HOLY GHOST, In Tongues, or In our Heavenly Language whichever way we choose to refer to it, we are praying beyond the limited capacity of our human weaknesses. We are totally trusting HOLY SPIRIT to use our cooperative and submitted regenerated human spirit, along with our tongue to release things into the earth that assist in fulfilling the will of GOD, and bringing forth the plans of GOD in the earth. How empowering it is to know that we are active participants in GOD'S plan for the world.

For many years I have considered myself a man of prayer. I would often pray in HOLY SPIRIT for the sake of going beyond my flesh. I always felt somewhat limited when I pray in my understanding. I would run out of words and literally get tired. I have encountered very few people who are able to pray for an extended period of time in their humanity, effectively. It happens that there are three anointed women who I characterize as having, "grace to pray." One of them is an Apostle in Elmira, NY, the other is an Apostolic Prophet who is an associate traveling often to the Island of Guadalupe, and the other is my biological daughter also an Ordained Minister. I mention them, because my personal interaction with them lets me know that there are others in the earth capable of praying in the understanding and have their words flow with an anointing like a mighty river of power. They never seem to run out of words when they pray. I enjoy prayer times with them so much. I personally am more effective when I pray in The SPIRIT while occasionally combining my understanding as necessary for the situation.

" For if I pray in an unknown tongue, my spirit prayeth, but my understanding is unfruitful. What is it then? I will pray with the spirit, and I will pray with the understanding also: I will sing with the spirit, and I will sing with the understanding also. Else when thou shalt bless with the spirit, how shall he that occupieth the room of the unlearned say Amen at thy giving of thanks, seeing he understandeth not what thou sayest? For thou verily givest thanks well, but the other is not edified. I thank my God, I speak with tongues more than ye all: Yet in the church I had rather speak five words with my understanding, that by my voice I might teach others also, than ten thousand words in an unknown tongue."
1 Corinthians 14:14-19 KJV

"For if I pray in an [unknown] tongue, my spirit [by the Holy Spirit within me] prays, but my mind is unproductive [it bears no fruit and helps nobody]. Then what am I to do? I will pray with my spirit [by the Holy Spirit that is within me], but I will also pray [intelligently] with my mind and understanding; I will sing with my spirit [by the Holy Spirit that is within me], but I will sing [intelligently] with my mind and understanding also. Otherwise, if you bless and render thanks with [your] spirit [thoroughly aroused by the Holy Spirit], how can anyone in the position of an outsider or he who is not gifted with [interpreting of unknown] tongues, say the Amen to your thanksgiving, since he does not know what you are saying? [I Chron. 16:36; Ps. 106:48.] To be sure, you may give thanks well (nobly), but the bystander is not edified [it does him no good]. I thank God that I speak in [strange] tongues (languages) more than any of you or all of you put together; Nevertheless, in public worship, I would rather say five words with my understanding and intelligently in order to instruct others, than ten thousand words in a [strange] tongue (language)."
1 Corinthians 14:14-19 AMPC

" For if I pray in tongues, my spirit is praying, but I don't understand what I am saying. Well then, what shall I do? I will pray in the spirit, and I will also pray in words I understand. I will sing in the spirit, and I will also sing in words I understand. For if you praise God only in the spirit, how can those who don't understand you praise God along with you? How can they join you in giving thanks when they don't understand

what you are saying? You will be giving thanks very well, but it won't strengthen the people who hear you. I thank God that I speak in tongues more than any of you. But in a church meeting I would rather speak five understandable words to help others than ten thousand words in an unknown language."
1 Corinthians 14:14-19 NLT

"So, when you pray in your private prayer language, don't hoard the experience for yourself. Pray for the insight and ability to bring others into that intimacy. If I pray in tongues, my spirit prays but my mind lies fallow, and all that intelligence is wasted. So what's the solution? The answer is simple enough. Do both. I should be spiritually free and expressive as I pray, but I should also be thoughtful and mindful as I pray. I should sing with my spirit, and sing with my mind. If you give a blessing using your private prayer language, which no one else understands, how can some outsider who has just shown up and has no idea what's going on know when to say "Amen"? Your blessing might be beautiful, but you have very effectively cut that person out of it. I'm grateful to God for the gift of praying in tongues that he gives us for praising him, which leads to wonderful intimacies we enjoy with him. I enter into this as much or more than any of you. But when I'm in a church assembled for worship, I'd rather say five words that everyone can understand and learn from than say ten thousand that sound to others like gibberish."
1 Corinthians 14:13-19 MSG

What a wonderful opportunity to have an effective prayer life. This is more than asking GOD to bless us and our family. Praying in Tongues is the greatest opportunity for effective prayer given to the believer. If that were not so, the enemy wouldn't spend so much energy to convince believers of the futility of Praying in The SPIRIT. HE uses lies in an attempt to convince believers that it is unnecessary, a lot of gibberish, or it is no longer applicable to our lives. So, if those arguments were true, then we who choose to pray this way are wasting our own time, and our prayers would be of no consequence. But ultimately, we have the word of GOD, which has lasted and affected the people of the earth for generations. It has and will continue to outlive every critic of the reality of the principles of our faith in GOD, and our allegiance to the King of Kings and the Lord of Lords.

One other benefit of HOLY SPIRIT prayer is found in the book of Jude:

"But ye, beloved, building up yourselves on your most holy faith, praying in the Holy Ghost,"
Jude 1:20 KJV

Building up our faith is of great necessity as we face the challenges in our relationship with GOD. Notice what Jude goes on to say, essentially he says, go deeper. Spend more time in fellowship with The FATHER. Go into the realm of HOLY SPIRIT and involve HIS presence in your daily lives. The Apostle Paul also says in his letters to the churches at Ephesus and Colossae:

" Speaking to yourselves in psalms and hymns and spiritual songs, singing and making melody in your heart to the Lord;"
Ephesians 5:19 KJV

"Let the word of Christ dwell in you richly in all wisdom; teaching and admonishing one another in psalms and hymns and spiritual songs, singing with grace in your hearts to the Lord."
Colossians 3:16 KJV

We must not allow ourselves to become good, "Social Christians." We live to impact the lives of those around us. Our assignment challenges us, as Jude verse 22 says, "...have compassion, making a difference;"

Making a difference requires us to impact others beyond our own human capacity. What changes the human heart is an undeniable spiritual experience with the presence of GOD, not the experience of the church alone. This can only be done when human beings have immersed themselves in the overwhelming, life changing presence of GOD through HOLY SPIRIT. JESUS said in John chapter 6, verse 44:

"No man can come to me, except the Father which hath sent me draw him: and I will raise him up at the last day."
John 6:44 KJV

"The only way people come to me is by the Father who sent me— he pulls on their hearts to embrace me. And those who are drawn to me, I will certainly raise them up in the last day."
John 6:44 TPT

"No one is able to come to Me unless the Father Who sent Me attracts and draws him and gives him the desire to come to Me, and [then] I will raise him up [from the dead] at the last day."
John 6:44 AMPC

This is a clear example of how vital it is for believers to spend time in the presence of GOD. The world we live in clearly requires manifested, tangible evidence of the reality of GOD. HOLY SPIRIT was dispatched to live within us, and operate in the earth through us to bring conviction to the hearts of men. As we pray in cooperation with HIM, we allow HIM to reach and influence lives in accordance with the will of GOD. Everything in the earth can be affected by the activity of praying in The SPIRIT. Our desire should always be that the will and the heart of GOD become tangibly evident in the lives of the people who live in the earth. It is also important to note that there is another form of prayer which we can embrace that allows us to become personal partners for change in the lives of specific people and specific situations in the activities of mankind.

Chapter 9

Intercession

"Wherefore he is able also to save them to the uttermost that come unto God by him, seeing he ever liveth to make intercession for them."
Hebrews 7:25 KJV

"So he is able to save fully from now throughout eternity, everyone who comes to God through him, because he lives to pray continually for them."
Hebrews 7:25 TPT

"Therefore He is able also to save to the uttermost (completely, perfectly, finally, and for all time and eternity) those who come to God through Him, since He is always living to make petition to God and intercede with Him and intervene for them."
Hebrews 7:25 AMPC

"Therefore he is able, once and forever, to save those who come to God through him. He lives forever to intercede with God on their behalf."
Hebrews 7:25 NLT

Without a doubt CHRIST JESUS is our greatest Advocate and Chief Intercessor before The Throne of GOD the FATHER! We can depend upon HIS commitment to us completing our earthly assignments successfully. I have great comfort and peace knowing that JESUS is stating my case before GOD, and living to remind The FATHER of my value to the Kingdom of Heaven.

It is a subject of some discussion as to whether there is one type of prayer which is more effective or important than another. However Intercession is the one form of prayer that allows us to become personal partners for change in the lives of specific people and specific situations in the activities of mankind. Just as JESUS lives to make intercession for us before The Father, we can make intercession in the earth for people and or situations.

"Who is he that condemneth? It is Christ that died, yea rather, that is risen again, who is even at the right hand of God, who also maketh intercession for us."
Romans 8:34 KJV

"Who then is left to condemn us? Certainly not Jesus, the Anointed One! For he gave his life for us, and even more than that, he has conquered death and is now risen, exalted, and enthroned by God at his right hand. So how could he possibly condemn us since he is continually praying for our triumph ?"
Romans 8:34 TPT

Intercede; Intercession, Intercessor, and Intercessory prayer are all terms which will be included in this chapter. Intercession or intercessory prayer is the act of praying to The FATHER on behalf of others.

"And he saw that there was no man, and wondered that there was no intercessor: therefore his arm brought salvation unto him; and his righteousness, it sustained him."
Isaiah 59:16 KJV

Intercession requires a personal commitment. It is largely a choice. However, there are times when HOLY SPIRIT will give us specific instructions to pray for a specific need at a specific time. It still requires the individual to say yes and obey HOLY SPIRIT'S instructions. There is a grace that is given to people who become intercessors. That grace is required to empower an individual. It emboldens them to unselfishly enter into the spirit realm, and strengthens them beyond any desire to give up.

Abraham chose to be the man to Intercede for Sodom and three other cities in the region. Abram's nephew Lot had taken his family and gone there in chapter 12 of Genesis. But the city was wicked, and GOD had pronounced judgment upon the city. However Abraham discovered that GOD was approachable, and willing to show mercy. So he humbly approached GOD on behalf of his relatives. However, the beautiful thing about GOD'S willingness to show mercy was that GOD agreed with Abraham that HE was willing to spare the whole city, if HE could find as few as 10 righteous people there. Since there were ultimately two other cities destroyed along with Sodom and Gomorrah, it is a demonstration of the power of one intercessor to see just how willing GOD is to be mercifully moved by the willingness of one person to intercede on behalf of another.

"And the men turned their faces from thence, and went toward Sodom: but Abraham stood yet before the Lord . And Abraham drew near, and said, Wilt thou also destroy the righteous with the wicked? Peradventure there be fifty righteous within the city: wilt thou also destroy and not spare the place for the fifty righteous that are therein? That be far from thee to do after this manner, to slay the righteous with the wicked: and that the righteous should be as the wicked, that be far from thee: Shall not the Judge of all the earth do right? And the Lord said, If I find in Sodom fifty righteous

within the city, then I will spare all the place for their sakes. And Abraham answered and said, Behold now, I have taken upon me to speak unto the Lord, which am but dust and ashes: Peradventure there shall lack five of the fifty righteous: wilt thou destroy all the city for lack of five? And he said, If I find there forty and five, I will not destroy it. And he spake unto him yet again, and said, Peradventure there shall be forty found there. And he said, I will not do it for forty's sake. And he said unto him, Oh let not the Lord be angry, and I will speak: Peradventure there shall thirty be found there. And he said, I will not do it, if I find thirty there. And he said, Behold now, I have taken upon me to speak unto the Lord: Peradventure there shall be twenty found there. And he said, I will not destroy it for twenty's sake. And he said, Oh let not the Lord be angry, and I will speak yet but this once: Peradventure ten shall be found there. And he said, I will not destroy it for ten's sake."
Genesis 18:22-32 KJV

This is part of the knowledge which I discovered years ago when the angels of the Lord intervened on behalf of my brother Tommy. Even though I used that experience to discuss Praying in The SPIRIT, it is also an example of the power of the prayer of Intercession as well as spiritual warfare. In doing so, I have learned that people all over the world have been and are continuing to be affected for the Kingdom, because Tommy is still alive, an Apostle of God, and has many years ahead to win souls and make disciples throughout the earth. Hallelujah to the Lamb of GOD!!!

I have also learned personally, and found agreement from many other intercessors around the world, that when we choose to intercede for the glory of God, we have to be willing to pay a personal price in ourselves so that the work of darkness can be disrupted and destroyed. Our choice to be an intercessor allows GOD'S work in the earth by HOLY SPIRIT and the angels to be successfully accomplished. But the work of darkness which is disrupted by our prayers, will impact us in physical, mental, and emotional ways. We literally put ourselves in between the enemy and the target of the attack. By so doing, we enter into a level of spiritual warfare that I will discuss in greater detail in another book.

Without a doubt, every time we intercede on behalf of a human individual, family group, or social entity, we are entering into a level of spiritual warfare. Make no mistake about it, the enemies of righteousness will do everything they can to prevent or stop us completely from our efforts at intercession. Intercessors are like front line warriors in the spiritual battle between Light and darkness.

There may be specific ways in which we address each form of prayer separately, but there is also a definite overlap between all three. While praying In Tongues is not an absolute necessity for Intercession, it does however, aid us in being able to assist in the work of Heaven in the lives or situations for which we stand in the gap. As we stand as conduits, or a bridge between the person or situation in need and the presence of GOD, we literally shield them from the onslaught of the enemy and enable the power of GOD to work within the process. Each form of prayer is disruptive to the work of darkness while at the same time empowering the agents of Heaven.

"For though we walk in the flesh, we do not war after the flesh: (For the weapons of our warfare are not carnal, but mighty through God

to the pulling down of strong holds;) Casting down imaginations, and every high thing that exalteth itself against the knowledge of God, and bringing into captivity every thought to the obedience of Christ; And having in a readiness to revenge all disobedience, when your obedience is fulfilled."
2 Corinthians 10:3-6 KJV

"For though we walk (live) in the flesh, we are not carrying on our warfare according to the flesh and using mere human weapons. For the weapons of our warfare are not physical [weapons of flesh and blood], but they are mighty before God for the overthrow and destruction of strongholds, [Inasmuch as we] refute arguments and theories and reasonings and every proud and lofty thing that sets itself up against the [true] knowledge of God; and we lead every thought and purpose away captive into the obedience of Christ (the Messiah, the Anointed One),"
2 Corinthians 10:3-5 AMPC

"The world is unprincipled. It's dog-eat-dog out there! The world doesn't fight fair. But we don't live or fight our battles that way—never have and never will. The tools of our trade aren't for marketing or manipulation, but they are for demolishing that entire massively corrupt culture. We use our powerful God-tools for smashing warped philosophies, tearing down barriers erected against the truth of God, fitting every loose thought and emotion and impulse into the structure of life shaped by Christ. Our tools are ready at hand for clearing the ground of every obstruction and building lives of obedience into maturity."
2 Corinthians 10:3-6 MSG

I will conclude by defining the difference between Intercession, and Spiritual Warfare. Intercession has a specific purpose or personal need which we target in our prayer time. Spiritual Warfare is much broader in its scope. We intercede primarily through specific prayer activity. Spiritual Warfare can be entered into through prayer alone, prayer and fasting (consecration), and praise and worship. There is also truth to the revelation that when we walk in the SPIRIT of GOD, and exhibit the love of GOD, we can be actively engaged in spiritual warfare at every moment of our lives. "Love never fails!"

"Finally, my brethren, be strong in the Lord, and in the power of his might. Put on the whole armour of God, that ye may be able to stand against the wiles of the devil. For we wrestle not against flesh and blood, but against principalities, against powers, against the rulers of the darkness of this world, against spiritual wickedness in high places. Wherefore take unto you the whole armour of God, that ye may be able to withstand in the evil day, and having done all, to stand. Stand therefore, having your loins girt about with truth, and having on the breastplate of righteousness; And your feet shod with the preparation of the gospel of peace; Above all, taking the shield of faith, wherewith ye shall be able to quench all the fiery darts of the wicked. And take the helmet of salvation, and the sword of the Spirit, which is the word of God: Praying always with all prayer and supplication in the Spirit, and watching thereunto with all perseverance and supplication for all saints;"
Ephesians 6:10-18 KJV

"In conclusion, be strong in the Lord [be empowered through your union with Him]; draw your strength from Him [that strength which His boundless might provides]. Put on God's whole armor [the armor of a heavy-armed soldier which God supplies], that you may be able successfully to stand up against [all] the strategies and the deceits of the devil. For we are not wrestling with flesh and blood [contending only with physical opponents], but against the despotisms, against the powers, against [the master spirits who are] the world rulers of this present darkness, against the spirit forces of wickedness in the heavenly (supernatural) sphere. Therefore put on God's complete armor, that you may be able to resist and stand your ground on the evil day [of danger], and, having done all [the crisis demands], to stand [firmly in your place]. Stand therefore [hold your ground], having tightened the belt of truth around your loins and having put on the breastplate of integrity and of moral rectitude and right standing with God, And having shod your feet in preparation [to face the enemy with the firm-footed stability, the promptness, and the readiness produced by the good news] of the

Gospel of peace. [Isa. 52:7.] Lift up over all the [covering] shield of saving faith, upon which you can quench all the flaming missiles of the wicked [one]. And take the helmet of salvation and the sword that the Spirit wields, which is the Word of God. Pray at all times (on every occasion, in every season) in the Spirit, with all [manner of] prayer and entreaty. To that end keep alert and watch with strong purpose and perseverance, interceding in behalf of all the saints (God's consecrated people)."
Ephesians 6:10-18 AMPC

"And that about wraps it up. God is strong, and he wants you strong. So take everything the Master has set out for you, well-made weapons of the best materials. And put them to use so you will be able to stand up to everything the Devil throws your way. This is no afternoon athletic contest that we'll walk away from and forget about in a couple of hours. This is for keeps, a life-or-death fight to the finish against the Devil and all his angels. Be prepared. You're up against far more than you can handle on your own. Take all the help you can get, every weapon God has issued, so that when it's all over but the shouting you'll still be on your feet. Truth, righteousness, peace, faith, and salvation are more than words. Learn how to apply them. You'll need them throughout your life. God's Word is an indispensable weapon. In the same way, prayer is essential in this ongoing warfare. Pray hard and long. Pray for your brothers and sisters. Keep your eyes open. Keep each other's spirits up so that no one falls behind or drops out."
Ephesians 6:10-18 MSG

Chapter 10

Travailing to Prevail

Travailing in the Spiritual Realm is a powerful combination of multiple forms of Prayer. It is part of the prayer of Intercession and also a part of Warfare Prayer. It is through the times of Travail that we are able to reach a point of breakthrough when dealing with challenging situations. It is also often the conduit through which ministry is established, activated, and released. We often face battles as in warfare which requires us to outlast and overpower the opposition so that lives are changed in a bloodline, a region, or a nation.

"Who hath heard such a thing? who hath seen such things? Shall the earth be made to bring forth in one day? or shall a nation be born at once? for as soon as Zion travailed, she brought forth her children."
Isaiah 66:8 KJV

"Who has heard of such a thing? Who has seen such things? Shall a land be born in one day? Or shall a nation be brought forth in a moment? For as soon as Zion was in labor, she brought forth her children."
Isaiah 66:8 AMPC

"Who has ever seen anything as strange as this? Who ever heard of such a thing? Has a nation ever been born in a single day? Has a country ever come forth in a mere moment? But by the time Jerusalem's birth pains begin, her children will be born."
Isaiah 66:8 NLT

"No one has ever heard of that happening; no one has ever seen that happen. In the same way no one ever saw a country begin in one day; no one has ever heard of a new nation beginning in one

moment. But Jerusalem will give birth to her children just as soon as she feels the birth pains".
Isaiah 66:8 NCV

"My little children, of whom I travail in birth again until Christ be formed in you,"
Galatians 4:19 KJV

"My children, I feel like a mother who is giving birth to you again. I will continue to feel that kind of pain until you become more completely like Christ."
Galatians 4:19 EASY

"You are my dear children, but I agonize in spiritual "labor pains" once again, until the Anointed One will be fully formed in your hearts!"
Galatians 4:19 TPT

"My dear children! Once again, just like a mother in childbirth, I feel the same kind of pain for you until Christ's nature is formed in you."
Galatians 4:19 GNTD

The Webster's dictionary meaning of the word, "Travail" means to engage in painful or laborious effort. It involves toil or a significant amount of physical exertion. It is a committed time of Prayer which utilizes the spiritual weapons available to us as GOD'S Sons and Daughters who as such are simultaneously citizens of the Kingdom of Heaven. The word of GOD, prayer, worship, and purposeful consecration are some of the spiritual resources available to us as we engage in times of travail.

In Isaiah, the Prophet declares that the establishment of the plan of GOD concerning Jerusalem will not happen without travail. Zion in the scriptures is generally a reference to Jerusalem geographically, and to the People of GOD corporately. So, the plan that GOD has for our lives will only be established through experiencing pain, effort, and some challenges. This is primarily due to the fact that GOD'S plan will always be opposed by an enemy and all of the forces of darkness at his disposal. Often spiritual leaders, intercessors, prayer warriors are called to stand in a place of purposeful "Spiritual Anchoring," whether that is extended times of Consecration, or a Five-Fold Minister physically remaining with a specific Church Congregation until there is a manifested "Break Through" in the spiritual attack being brought against the specific people or Church. This is not an accidental activity. Anchoring is an apostolic activity in which a Disciple of CHRIST JESUS under HOLY SPIRIT'S instructions makes a spiritual commitment to stay before the presence of GOD until a situation changes or is resolved in a tangible way. Travail will always produce results; first in the Spirit, and then in the natural. Sometimes a Pastor will be commanded to Minister on a certain subject and then combine the teaching and or preaching with a subsequent time of prayer until a breakthrough comes. The result will be physically seen and tangibly experienced by those affected by the situation which was the reason for the travail. So Isaiah tells the people, that this won't just happen. You won't see the promise, and you won't experience the breakthrough without enduring and overcoming challenges. But if you are faithful and committed, everything GOD promised will come to pass.

One example of travailing prayer was Hannah the mother of the Prophet Samuel who was the last Judge of Israel before the time of a royal class of leaders. Hannah was married, but had not been able to have children. Her husband also had another wife who did have children, and this became a major issue for Hannah. So Hannah eventually went before the LORD and cried out of her heart in the midst of her mental anguish and emotional pain until she got the attention of Eli the priest who lived in the temple of the LORD. When Eli observed her crying out to GOD in her pain, he only saw her lips moving but heard no sound. This led him to assume that she was drunk in the House of The LORD. After Hannah explained to Eli her situation, he declared to her prophetically that GOD had heard her cry and had granted her petition. So within the time of pregnancy and birthing, Samuel was born. So, it wasn't necessary for the prayer we saw to be a long one, but it is significant to know that Hannah had been in a time of personal travail much longer than the time frame in the first chapter of Samuel. But the end result was a breakthrough which manifested a tangible result named Samuel.   Hannah was willing to travail, and Hannah prevailed.

The Apostle Paul in his letter to the Galatian Church writes concerning their lack of total commitment to the principles of their new relationship with GOD. They were wavering because they were being influenced by the old social contacts coming from the people with whom they previously associated. So Paul reminds them of their position with GOD, and tells them that he is, "anchoring himself" spiritually and travailing again in prayer with and for them, until they begin to manifest the nature and characteristics of CHRIST, (The Anointed One and HIS Anointing.) It was clear that the prayers which he was generally praying for them were not enough to create a solid foundation in their relationship with GOD. So he tells them that he is committed to "Travailing," again in prayer for them until the life and character of CHRIST becomes a tangible reality in their lives. Often we can be committed to regularly praying for someone or a situation, but the object of our attention in prayer is not cooperative with our efforts. They may not be strong enough personally to deal with the things oppressing their life on their own. So our willingness to Travail in prayer for them gives a supernatural boost to the condition. I have often used travailing prayer for individuals who have had drug addictions, marital issues, or challenges between parents and children. I personally experienced a breakthrough for an, "adopted" brother who was facing jail time, and watched the power of GOD deliver him from facing more than over 20 years in prison, to absolutely no jail time whatsoever. He was given probation and walked away.   The power of GOD is continuing to enlarge his life to this day. Travailing Prayer is a costly form of prayer just as intercession is. The very idea of travailing implies a painful experience. So when we are called to travail for a specific cause, it is generally something that will impact many people and also a necessary activity, allowing that people to experience the desired result.

The ultimate purpose for travailing in prayer is to produce a tangible victory as a result of our efforts. That is proof that we have, "Prevailed." Prevailing only requires that we remain anchored in our time of travail. Paul assures us in 2 Corinthians 2.14:

" Now thanks be unto God, which always causeth us to triumph in Christ, and maketh manifest the savour of his knowledge by us in every place."
2 Corinthians 2:14 KJV

"But thanks be to God, Who in Christ always leads us in triumph [as trophies of Christ's victory] and through us spreads and makes evident the fragrance of the knowledge of God everywhere,"
2 Corinthians 2:14 AMPC

We have been empowered to walk in Triumph as children of GOD. We are encouraged to demonstrate that triumph as we live victoriously in the earth. As such, that triumph is also a celebratory example of that which was manifested in the earth when JESUS was resurrected from the grave, to the Heavenly position of CHRIST. The ultimate manifestation of that Prevailing victory was the ascension of CHRIST JESUS upon the cloud rising into the Heavenly sphere. So it is, that if we will commit ourselves to Travailing in Prayer, we are destined for a breakthrough outcome which will demonstrate our Prevailing authority "In CHRIST JESUS." Thank GOD for the ability with which HE empowers us to win in every situation. We can win for The Kingdom of Heaven, and ultimately prevail to release others as well.

Chapter 11

Warfare Prayer

The human race is made up of three part beings. We are a Spirit, we have a Soul, and we live in a Body. This is a fundamental truth that all Christians must acknowledge. If this truth is not embraced, interaction and intimacy with The Heavenly Trinity contained within the Person of the Godhead is impossible. The totality of our successful existence in the earth is dependent upon a person's ability and choice to acknowledge this reality. We are spirit beings. Our body is an earth suit, a shell which is created to contain our soul and spirit. At birth, we enter the earth as spirit beings which have been implanted by GOD in the womb of a woman who becomes our mother.

"Then the word of the Lord came unto me, saying, Before I formed thee in the belly I knew thee; and before thou camest forth out of the womb I sanctified thee, and I ordained thee a prophet unto the nations."
Jeremiah 1:4-5 KJV

"God spoke to me. 'I knew you even before I made your body inside your mother's body. I chose you before you were born. I decided that you must be a prophet to all the countries in the world,' he said."
Jeremiah 1:4-5 EASY

"The LORD said to me, "I chose you before I gave you life, and before you were born I selected you to be a prophet to the nations."
Jeremiah 1:4-5 GNB

"The Lord spoke his word to me, "Before I formed you in the womb, I knew you. Before you were born, I set you apart for my holy purpose. I appointed you to be a prophet to the nations."
Jeremiah 1:4-5 GW

"And the word of Yahweh came to me, saying, "Before I formed you in the womb I knew you, and before you came out from the womb I consecrated you; I appointed you as a prophet to the nations."
Jeremiah 1:4-5 LEB

"This is what God said: "Before I shaped you in the womb, I knew all about you. Before you saw the light of day, I had holy plans for you: A prophet to the nations— that's what I had in mind for you."
Jeremiah 1:1-5 MSG

"The Lord spoke his word to me, saying: "Before I made you in your mother's womb, I chose you. Before you were born, I set you apart for a special work. I appointed you as a prophet to the nations."
Jeremiah 1:4-5 NCV

"The Lord spoke his word to me, saying: "Before I made you in your mother's womb, I chose you. Before you were born, I set you apart for a special work. I appointed you as a prophet to the nations."
Jeremiah 1:4-5 NCV

"And there is a word of Jehovah unto me, saying, 'Before I form thee in the belly, I have known thee; and before thou comest forth from the womb I have separated thee, a prophet to nations I have made thee.'"
Jeremiah 1:4-5 YLT1898

The context of this scripture clearly indicates that this verse is a testimony of Jeremiah in which he shares an interaction between himself and GOD. However, the theological revelation for our faith is that GOD knows us before HE creates us in the earth. HE has a relationship with us which preexists our birth. HE also, gives us a purpose which HE desires for us to fulfill. The implication of these words is that we are created and birthed with a purpose, even though we may not walk in that purpose. I want to tell you this; purpose is attached to every being that exists in the earth. All we have to do is to allow GOD to reveal the purpose through HOLY SPIRIT.

However, it is essential to realize that we have an adversary who will oppose us and seek to disrupt our pursuit of GOD and HIS purpose for our lives. Since the opposition is spiritually created, it becomes necessary to engage the adversary on a spiritual level. Some people may wonder how they will be able to overcome unseen spiritual forces. The powerful truth which answers that question is found in the revelation that GOD equipped us with the ability to operate both in a physical realm as well as a spiritual one. Since HE is spirit and created us in HIS image, HE has given us access to the spirit realm as well.

The Bible lets us know from the beginning that we have been made in the image of GOD.

"So God created man in his own image, in the image of God created he him; male and female created he them."
Genesis 1:27 KJV

"So God created human beings in his own image. In the image of God he created them; male and female he created them."
Genesis 1:27 NLT

Since we are created in the image of GOD, the only thing we need to do, is to understand what that image is. There must be significance to this scripture.

"For God is Spirit, so those who worship him must worship in spirit and in truth."
John 4:24 NLT

"God is a Spirit: and they that worship him must worship him in spirit and in truth."
John 4:24 KJV

"God is a Spirit (a spiritual Being) and those who worship Him must worship Him in spirit and in truth (reality)."
John 4:24 AMPC

GOD is Spirit. HE created us in HIS image, and HE did so knowing that HE was going to make HIS power and ability available to us. HE is our father. We who accept that truth embrace HIM as Our FATHER GOD. If we are in HIS image then a living Spirit JEHOVAH created us to live victoriously as HIS children.

"Furthermore we have had fathers of our flesh which corrected us, and we gave them reverence: shall we not much rather be in subjection unto the Father of spirits, and live?"
Hebrews 12:9 KJV

"Moreover, we have had earthly fathers who disciplined us and we yielded [to them] and respected [them for training us]. Shall we not much more cheerfully submit to the Father of spirits and so [truly] live?"
Hebrews 12:9 AMPC

"We have all had fathers here on earth who disciplined us, and we respected them. So it is even more important that we accept discipline from the Father of our spirits so we will have life."
Hebrews 12:9 NCV

"Furthermore, we have had human fathers, and they corrected us, and we gave them reverence. Shall we not much more be subject to the Father of spirits and live?"
Hebrews 12:9 MEV

"Since we respected our earthly fathers who disciplined us, shouldn't we submit even more to the discipline of the Father of our spirits, and live forever?"
Hebrews 12:9 NLT

The Father of spirits is the father who created us as HIS children. We are spirit, we live in a physical reality contained within a physical body, but we are all individuals. It is our soul which gives us that individuality and makes us the unique person that we are. As we establish the individuality of our existence, we need to understand that our physical attributes are a representation of GOD'S spiritual attributes. GOD is not just an ethereal energy force. He is a real being, existing in a spiritual realm which contains our natural existence. Our physical appendages come from the image of GOD'S spiritual being. GOD is a spiritual person. HE has a personality. HIS personality is the model of perfection which we strive to attain. GOD is an omnipotent being, possessing all existing power; omniscient, all knowing of everything that can be known; and omnipresent, existing everywhere at all times. So too, HE has given us a personality. Our soul is our unique identity. Our soul contains mental capability, imagination, creativity, and emotions.

"And the very God of peace sanctify you wholly; and I pray God your whole spirit and soul and body be preserved blameless unto the coming of our Lord Jesus Christ."
1 Thessalonians 5:23 KJV

"And may the God of peace Himself sanctify you through and through [separate you from profane things, make you pure and wholly consecrated to God]; and may your spirit and soul and body be preserved sound and complete [and found] blameless at the

coming of our Lord Jesus Christ (the Messiah)."
1 Thessalonians 5:23 AMPC

"Now, may the God of peace and harmony set you apart, making you completely holy. And may your entire being—spirit, soul, and body—be kept completely flawless in the appearing of our Lord Jesus, the Anointed One."
1 Thessalonians 5:23 TPT

Each of the three parts of our being enables us to function effectively in the earth realm. Each part of our being also has challenges which must be addressed throughout our lifetime. There are health challenges which we deal with physically, things that have an effect on us mentally, and the events which occur and effect our emotions. Most of these activities originate in the spirit realm. It is through the activity of our regenerated, (Born-Again) human spirit that GOD gave mankind the ability to successfully overcome the challenges the other parts of our being face every day. When the time comes, and our body is no longer able to provide a place for our spirit to live, the spirit returns to GOD, and the destination of our soul is what is left to be determined.

"Then shall the dust return to the earth as it was: and the spirit shall return unto God who gave it".
Ecclesiastes 12:7 KJV

"You will turn back into the dust of the earth again, but your spirit will return to God who gave it."
Ecclesiastes 12:7 NCV

It is through the redemptive work of JESUS CHRIST that we are able to determine the eternal destination of our soul. If we accept the sacrificial death, burial, and victorious resurrection of JESUS the first born son of GOD, then we ensure that our soul will have an eternal fellowship with GOD the FATHER of our spirit. This is the reason that the enemy fights so hard to keep us from making a personal decision to accept CHRIST JESUS as the Saviour of our soul. Once our soul is secured by this decision, we begin the process of increasing our spiritual effectiveness and value to Heaven's Kingdom.

There are two kingdoms which we deal with. These kingdoms wage an unending spiritual battle for the eternal destination of the souls of men. The two kingdoms are the Kingdom of HIS dear Son and the kingdom of darkness.

'Who hath delivered us from the power of darkness, and hath translated us into the kingdom of his dear Son:"
Colossians 1:13 KJV

" [The Father] has delivered and drawn us to Himself out of the control and the dominion of darkness and has transferred us into the kingdom of the Son of His love,"
Colossians 1:13 AMPC

"For he has rescued us from the kingdom of darkness and transferred us into the Kingdom of his dear Son,"
Colossians 1:13 NLT

"God has freed us from the power of darkness, and he brought us into the kingdom of his dear Son."
Colossians 1:13 NCV

"God rescued us from dead-end alleys and dark dungeons. He's set us up in the kingdom of the Son he loves so much, the Son who got us out of the pit we were in, got rid of the sins we were doomed to keep repeating."

Colossians 1:13-14 MSG

The FATHER changed our spiritual residence, and gave us a place of residence which is appropriate for HIS children. Our citizenship in this powerful and righteous kingdom gives us the opportunity to have a great impact on the activities which occur in the earth. It is the possibility of us embracing the opportunity to positively affect GOD'S pan, and have a negative effect on the enemy's plan which makes us a danger to the kingdom of darkness. It is this possibility of attacks to his kingdom which satan has feared from the time of JESUS' earthly existence. The enemy knows that The FATHER has given us the authority and the power to win any and every battle we engage in to bring about our enemy's destruction. This is spiritual warfare. This is what we face even if we have not become willing and conscious participants in battle against the enemy; the enemy is committed to destroying us. The kingdom of darkness enters into purposeful spiritual warfare against us from the time of our birth. The enemy hates mankind because we have the opportunity to live eternally with The FATHER. Our enemy chose darkness, evil, and opposition to the plan and authority of The FATHER. SO, the possibility of a human being choosing to join the Kingdom of Heaven is something that darkness will always fight. We are marked for destruction by the darkness that exists in the spiritual realm. However, we have been given the tools and the opportunity to be victorious through choosing to actively live as citizens of GOD'S Kingdom.

This is the reason for warfare prayer. Remember the truth which HOLY SPIRIT revealed to me a few years ago: "Your tongue speaking the word of GOD in faith is the most powerful force on the earth." When we pray in opposition to the darkness, we are able to empower Heavenly beings to operate on behalf of GOD'S Kingdom. More specifically, the angels of GOD are strengthened and the Hosts of Heaven are released as they minister according to the assignment they've been given.

"Bless the Lord , ye his angels, that excel in strength, that do his commandments, hearkening unto the voice of his word. Bless ye the Lord , all ye his hosts; ye ministers of his, that do his pleasure." Psalms 103:20-21 KJV

"Bless (affectionately, gratefully praise) the Lord, you His angels, you mighty ones who do His commandments, hearkening to the voice of His word. Bless (affectionately, gratefully praise) the Lord, all you His hosts, you His ministers who do His pleasure." Psalm 103:20-21 AMPC

"Praise the Lord , you angels, you mighty ones who carry out his plans, listening for each of his commands. Yes, praise the Lord , you armies of angels who serve him and do his will!" Psalms 103:20-21 NLT

So we know that the Hosts of Heaven exist to fulfill the will of GOD. Angels listen to hear GOD'S voice. So, when we pray the word of GOD, whether consciously or through warfare prayer, we become the voice of GOD in the earth. We provide support and strength to the spiritual forces operating on behalf of the will of GOD. Everything they do is done within the spirit realm. Our greatest opposition exists within that realm. So then it is there that we are given the opportunity to have the greatest impact on the activities of our life as well as the lives of others. The enemies we face are not physical. Many times in the course of ministering, I have said to believers, "People are not your enemy, spirits of darkness are." As I write this chapter, I am sure that I will write a separate book on the operation of the spirit realm. People can be influenced, manipulated, and controlled by spiritual forces whose goal it is to cause havoc in the earth as well as negatively impacting the lives of believers. Those dark spiritual forces are specifically assigned to the lives of the children of GOD through their bloodlines as well as their associations to gain access to and create negative issues in our lives.

"For we wrestle not against flesh and blood, but against principalities, against powers, against the rulers of the darkness of this world, against spiritual wickedness in high places."
Ephesians 6:12 KJV

"For we are not wrestling with flesh and blood [contending only with physical opponents], but against the despotisms, against the powers, against [the master spirits who are] the world rulers of this present darkness, against the spirit forces of wickedness in the heavenly (supernatural) sphere."
Ephesians 6:12 AMPC

"Our fight is not against people on earth but against the rulers and authorities and the powers of this world's darkness, against the spiritual powers of evil in the heavenly world."
Ephesians 6:12 NCV

"For we are not fighting against flesh-and-blood enemies, but against evil rulers and authorities of the unseen world, against mighty powers in this dark world, and against evil spirits in the heavenly places".
Ephesians 6:12 NLT

So while we are living a life in an effort to advance the Kingdom of Heaven, the enemy is operating against our efforts. When we pray in The Spirit we have immediate and direct confrontation in the spirit realm. However, we have to understand that there is a hierarchy in both natural as well as spiritual kingdoms. As the scriptures above indicate we are clearly fighting spiritual enemies that operate under different levels of authority. Our greatest operational force is spiritual beings that minister on our behalf because of our citizenship position as children of The Father GOD. Angels are our personal helpers in the spirit realm. They are created to facilitate the will of GOD, which they do with our assistance in prayer. As we pray in The Spirit we release angelic activity and build up a fortress strengthening the light.

" But to which of the angels said he at any time, Sit on my right hand, until I make thine enemies thy footstool? Are they not all ministering spirits, sent forth to minister for them who shall be heirs of salvation?"
Hebrews 1:13-14 KJV

"Are not the angels all ministering spirits (servants) sent out in the service [of God for the assistance] of those who are to inherit salvation?"
Hebrews 1:14 AMPC

"Therefore, angels are only servants—spirits sent to care for people who will inherit salvation."
Hebrews 1:14 NLT

"All the angels are spirits who serve God and are sent to help those who will receive salvation".
Hebrews 1:14 NCV

This war is a fixed fight. The outcome has been predetermined. What's left is for the enemy to attempt to have those of us who believe in GOD join him in an eternal separation from GOD, or for us to maintain our relationship with GOD and live eternally with HIM. That is why I pray. I know that when I pray the word of GOD, HIS will is being done. When I agree with other believers, Heavenly forces are supercharged on assignment to accomplish what we pray. I pray in spiritual warfare specifically targeting the forces of the darkness of this world because my voice is authorized to release the word and power of GOD, allowing Heavenly forces access to the earth realm. Lives are impacted; situations are turned from bad to good. The outcome of the decision making process for us or others for whom we are interceding is turned in our favor. We don't have to choose to utilize warfare prayer, but that will not stop the enemy of our soul from waging war against us. The war for our soul's eternal position is not dependent upon any Ecclesiastical titles. We were marked for increased attack from the demonic spirits of darkness the moment we chose to acknowledge JESUS as the Christ, as the Saviour of our souls. We embrace HIM as the Lord of our life, and submit to the will of GOD for ourselves. The enemy doesn't like you or I or any other believer. However the enemy is terrified that a believer will become aware of the power and authority we have been given to operate against the kingdom of darkness, through the authority of our spiritual position in CHRIST JESUS.

In February of 2009, I had an encounter with GOD during a time of 40 days of consecration. I would fast and pray to increase my personal ability to fellowship intimately with GOD. That is when HE told me how valuable those who pray are to the work of the Kingdom of Heaven.

"I have plenty of people who are willing to preach, but not enough people who are willing to pray."

Subsequent to that encounter, in November of 2011, I had an experience while praying In Tongues. As I was praying one night in agreement with a partner of mine Carla, who is from Mt. Airy, NC; I personally witnessed an angelic warrior armored in gold which vibrated through the wall of the house on the left side of the room in which I was praying. The Angel was as tall as the room from ceiling to floor. The Angel vibrated through the wall becoming visible for an instant long enough for me to recognize that this was a real being. Then immediately the Angel flashed through the room, through my body, and passed through the wall on my right and out of the home. There followed a host of angelic beings which came through the wall moving consistently faster, each one also covered in gold and moving until it appeared as though a long stream of bright golden light was passing through the house and through my body as I was praying. For a moment I wondered if I should stop praying, but in that moment I heard Holy Spirit say to me, "Don't stop praying Walter. The angels are utilizing your prayer as a person would drive into a filling station. They are being strengthened to complete their assignment while you are praying. I have prayer portals throughout the earth where the prayers of GOD'S people in this realm strengthen the angels to operate in the spirit realm. This is one of the most important reasons that I have called you to pray. The lives of people around the earth are impacted when you commit to pray."

There are specific things that I pray during a time of warfare. I have no doubt that as HOLY SPIRIT leads, the subject or issue I pray about are taken care of. Prayer always causes change. So, the Kingdom of Heaven is recruiting prayer warriors. I often hear ministers teach or preach on the subject of spiritual warfare and I realize from their teaching that they are not personally engaged in the subject as an activity. Spiritual warfare marks a believer for increased attack against our life. This attack from the enemy also exposes vulnerabilities and weaknesses in our relationship with GOD. However, though these facts are true, they are nothing to be afraid of. The love of GOD will strengthen us and cover us beyond any area of weakness and protect our lives personally, our family, and covenant connections as we operate in obedience to HOLY SPIRIT'S strategies. We have already been declared victorious, more than conquerors through the power and love of JESUS CHRIST. HALLELUJA!!! The battles we fight are fixed. It is the assault which we wage against the darkness which rattles disrupts, and ultimately destroys the plans, plots, and tactics of the enemy. There is no reason to fear. Being on the frontlines is an honor in the Kingdom of Heaven. I encourage you to seek the LORD as to whether you have been chosen to engage the enemy, and take the battle to the gates of hell. I encourage everyone to enlist.

Chapter 12

Prayer and Fasting

"And when he came to his disciples, he saw a great multitude about them, and the scribes questioning with them. And straightway all the people, when they beheld him, were greatly amazed, and running to him saluted him. And he asked the scribes, What question ye with them? And one of the multitude answered and said, Master, I have brought unto thee my son, which hath a dumb spirit; And wheresoever he taketh him, he teareth him: and he foameth, and gnasheth with his teeth, and pineth away: and I spake to thy disciples that they should cast him out; and they could not. He answereth him, and saith, O faithless generation, how long shall I be with you? how long shall I suffer you? bring him unto me. And they brought him unto him: and when he saw him, straightway the spirit tare him; and he fell on the ground, and wallowed foaming. And he asked his father, How long is it ago since this came unto him? And he said, Of a child. And ofttimes it hath cast him into the fire, and into the waters, to destroy him: but if thou canst do any thing, have compassion on us, and help us. Jesus said unto him, If thou canst believe, all things are possible to him that believeth. And straightway the father of the child cried out, and said with tears, Lord, I believe; help thou mine unbelief. When Jesus saw that the people came running together, he rebuked the foul spirit, saying unto him, Thou dumb and deaf spirit, I charge thee, come out of him, and enter no more into him. And the spirit cried, and rent him sore, and came out of him: and he was as one dead; insomuch that many said, He is dead. But Jesus took him by the hand, and lifted him up; and he arose. And when he was come into the house, his disciples asked him privately, Why could not we cast him out? And he said unto them, This kind can come forth by nothing, but by prayer and fasting."
Mark 9:14-29 KJV

"When they came back down the mountain to the other disciples, they saw a huge crowd around them, and the religion scholars cross-examining them. As soon as the people in the crowd saw Jesus, admiring excitement stirred them. They ran and greeted him. He asked, "What's going on? What's all the commotion?" A man out of the crowd answered, "Teacher, I brought my mute son, made speechless by a demon, to you. Whenever it seizes him, it throws him to the ground. He foams at the mouth, grinds his teeth, and goes stiff as a board. I told your disciples, hoping they could deliver him, but they couldn't." Jesus said, "What a generation! No sense of God! How many times do I have to go over these things? How much longer do I have to put up with this? Bring the boy here." They brought him. When the demon saw Jesus, it threw the boy into a seizure, causing him to writhe on the ground and foam at the mouth. He asked the boy's father, "How long has this been going on?" "Ever since he was a little boy. Many times it pitches him into fire or the river to do away with him. If you can do anything, do it. Have a heart and help us!" Jesus said, "If? There are no 'ifs' among believers. Anything can happen." No sooner were the words out of his mouth than the father cried, "Then I believe. Help me with my doubts!" Seeing that the crowd was forming fast, Jesus gave the vile spirit its marching orders: "Dumb and deaf spirit, I command you—Out of him, and stay out!" Screaming, and with much thrashing about, it left. The boy was pale as a corpse, so people started saying, "He's dead." But Jesus, taking his hand, raised him. The boy stood up. After arriving back home, his disciples cornered Jesus and asked, "Why couldn't we throw the demon out?" He answered, "There is no way to get rid of this kind of demon except by prayer."
Mark 9:14-29 MSG

I have wrestled with whether to mix the thoughts of this chapter in with a couple of the previous chapters. However, the overwhelming impact of this area of my individual prayer life cannot be overstated. Therefore, I felt a peace that HOLY SPIRIT would provide insight to me as I share what this prayer activity has meant and continues to mean to my life.

From my earliest memories of the teachings of The Church, I was taught as much, if not more, about prayer and fasting, as about anything other than our redemption through CHRIST JESUS. These two words hold the key to the manifestation of victorious power which demonstrated in the scriptures noted here are still relevant today. As I have noted before, almost all of these chapters could have a separate book devoted to the full discussion of it. So, I will give this area as much attention as HOLY SPIRIT allows.

Since all of the previous material has been devoted to the importance and relevance of prayer, what I want to address is the specific relevance of what happens when these two spiritual, "weapons of our warfare," are purposely combined in an effort to experience at least the same level of results as occurred in the Bible. I am writing from the perspective of someone who believes in our spiritual authority described in the word of GOD. So then, since we have been given power and authority over all the power of the enemy,"(Luke 10.19) it's important to recognize that this same JESUS described the necessity of an additional level of power which is required to cast out manifested demonic activity. It is this additional power level which after HE demonstrates in the presence of HIS Disciples, JESUS describes as only being made available through prayer and fasting. While fasting is clearly not imperative for the pursuit of a personal life relationship with The FATHER, it clearly is necessary to exercise this level of spiritual authority. This scriptural reference indicates that only someone who has practiced prayer and fasting is able to exercise a level of power and authority sufficient for the casting out of demons.

Clearly, it doesn't just happen, and it's not enough just to be a believer. However I am also compelled to point out that there is an expectation in the word that there is an existent expectation that all believers will pray and fast at some point in their relationship with The FATHER.

"Moreover when ye fast, be not, as the hypocrites, of a sad countenance: for they disfigure their faces, that they may appear unto men to fast. Verily I say unto you, They have their reward."
Matthew 6:16 KJV

"Whenever you pray, be sincere and not like the pretenders who love the attention they receive while praying before others in the meetings and on street corners. Believe me, they've already received in full their reward. But whenever you pray, go into your innermost chamber and be alone with Father God, praying to him in secret. And your Father, who sees all you do, will reward you openly. When you pray, there is no need to repeat empty phrases, praying like those who don't know God, for they expect God to hear them because of their many words. There is no need to imitate them, since your Father already knows what you need before you ask him. Pray like this: 'Our Father, dwelling in the heavenly realms, may the glory of your name be the center on which our lives turn. Manifest your kingdom realm, and cause your every purpose to be fulfilled on earth, just as it is fulfilled in heaven. We acknowledge you as our Provider of all we need each day. Forgive us the wrongs we have done as we ourselves release forgiveness to those who have wronged us. Rescue us every time we face tribulation and set us free from evil. For you are the King who rules with power and glory forever. Amen.' " And when you pray , make sure you forgive the faults of others so that your Father in heaven will also forgive you. But if you withhold forgiveness from others, your Father withholds forgiveness from you." "When you fast, don't look like those who pretend to be spiritual. They want everyone to know they're fasting, so they appear in public looking miserable, gloomy, and disheveled. Believe me, they've already received their reward in full. When you fast, don't let it be obvious, but instead, wash your face and groom yourself and realize that your Father in the secret place is the one who is watching all that you do in secret and will continue to reward you openly."
Matthew 6:5-18 TPT

One word in this scripture cannot be ignored, "When." The word when is consistent throughout the various versions of the BIBLE. So clearly, prayer and fasting is an activity which every believer is expected to participate in at some point.

I never see any indication in the word of GOD where JJESUS ever did anything unnecessarily. JESUS always did what HE did so that HE could demonstrate for HIS disciples that the authority of The FATHER was active and alive within him. It also demonstrates for all believers who would follow, how our humanity can be impacted by the knowledge of how to exercise power over darkness from the spirit realm. JESUS wanted to show us that demonic possession and operation in the earth realm doesn't just happen without the cooperation of the host, the ability to demonstrate authority over them is not accidental; it must be done on purpose. The combination of Prayer and Fasting is a purposeful activity with demonstrable results.

I often have people who are aspiring to ministry ask me why I pray so much. I think of the activities of those who were used by GOD in the Old Testament, as well as the Disciples and the Apostles in the New Testament and I come up with one answer; we are called to glorify GOD in the earth. To do so effectively, there will be instances when we are challenged to demonstrate the authority and power available to us through our relationship with GOD through CHRIST JESUS. This demonstrable ability demands that we have an experiential knowledge of Prayer and Fasting. The more intimate we are with GOD, the more we will be available for HIS purpose. If we are living to fulfill HIS purpose, then we make choices which actively demonstrate HIS power in our lives. It's your choice how close you become to GOD. Two things are clear to me in this moment:

"Draw nigh to God, and he will draw nigh to you...."
James 4:8 KJV

"… but the people that do know their God shall be strong, and do exploits."
Daniel 11:32 KJV

" but the people who know their God shall prove themselves strong and shall stand firm and do exploits [for God]."
Daniel 11:32 AMPC

Chapter 13

Prayers That I Pray Daily

I have to say that this book is very hard to end. Everything in my life revolves around my intimate fellowship with My Heavenly Father. I have spent parts of the last four years writing this book. Many people close to me know some of what has taken place in my life over the past few years. However, I can confess in this moment that none of the things which have brought transition and change in my reality have altered my commitment to and longing for the presence of The FATHER. So as I was preparing for the publishing of this material, and thinking that it was complete, HOLY SPIRIT spoke to me and instructed me to conclude with a few scriptural references concerning prayer which give me continual strength and encouragement. In case I haven't made it clear to you at this point, I want to say it this way. The FATHER is always with us wherever we are. When we pray we are not embarking on a journey in search of HIM. HE promised never to leave us or forsake us, and HE always keeps HIS promises. So, HE is always ready and waiting when we show up in the time we make for prayer. Not only that, I pray that you are filled to overflowing with the joy which flows from HIM every time we show up in HIS presence. I pray that you become fully aware of your positional authority as a child of The Most High GOD, "El Elyon," and that the wisdom to utilize that authority skillfully is activated as you spend time receiving from HIM.   You can never be, too unclean, never too unworthy, never stay away, too long for GOD not to love spending time with you when you show up. So, just show up. Purposely make time just to stop and let HIM know that you believe enough to hope that HE will be aware of your effort. You are HIS child. HE is your Father. Nothing thrills me more to this day than having my Grandson knock on my door and come boldly into the room giving me a clear indication that he wants to spend some time with his Grandfather. Even though my children are adults, and living their own lives, a contact with either of the three of them just strengthens and encourages me. Every interaction with them is proof that my life has been purposeful and valuable. Every time we acknowledge that we are children of GOD by showing up to spend time with HIM as our Father, we let the natural and spiritual realm know that HIS love for us and HIS purpose for us hold's great value.

I'm full to overflowing with such immense joy and thanksgiving for having the opportunity to fully access the presence of The FATHER. Through my prayer life, I am unquestionably aware that HIS love for me is unwavering, and unconditional. Prayer is without a doubt the most powerful and effective spiritual weapon we can use in conjunction with the word of GOD, and our faith in GOD. The little boy, whose mother took him to noonday prayer meeting more than 50 years ago, still gets excited about the commitment of my mother and the effort that it took to get to that home every day to pray. How amazing is it that all I have to do is stop and ignore everything else around me right where I am and know that HE will spend time with me right here. This is the one thing that changes everything for me. I live to pray.

Just keep asking GOD:

 "And he said unto them, Which of you shall have a friend, and shall go unto him at midnight, and say unto him, Friend, lend me three loaves; For a friend of mine in his journey is come to me, and I have nothing to set before him?   And he from within shall answer and say, Trouble me not: the door is now shut, and my children are with me in bed; I cannot rise and give thee. I say unto you, Though he will not rise and give him, because he is his friend, yet because of his importunity he will rise and give him as many as he needeth. And I say unto you, Ask, and it shall be given you; seek, and ye shall find; knock, and it shall be opened unto you.   For every one that asketh receiveth; and he that seeketh findeth; and to him that knocketh it shall be opened.   If a son shall ask bread of any of you that is a father, will he give him a stone? or if he ask a fish, will he for a fish give him a serpent?   Or if he shall ask an egg, will he offer him a scorpion?   If ye then, being evil, know how to give good gifts unto your children: how much more shall your heavenly Father give the Holy Spirit to them that ask him?"
Luke 11:5-13 KJV

"And He said to them, Which of you who has a friend will go to him at midnight and will say to him, Friend, lend me three loaves [of bread], For a friend of mine who is on a journey has just come, and I have nothing to put before him; And he from within will answer, Do not disturb me; the door is now closed, and my children are with me in bed; I cannot get up and supply you [with anything]? I tell you, although he will not get up and supply him anything because he is his friend, yet because of his shameless persistence and insistence he will get up and give him as much as he needs. So I say to you, Ask and keep on asking and it shall be given you; seek and keep on seeking and you shall find; knock and keep on knocking and the door shall be opened to you. For everyone who asks and keeps on asking receives; and he who seeks and keeps on seeking finds; and to him who knocks and keeps on knocking, the door shall be

opened. What father among you, if his son asks for a loaf of bread, will give him a stone; or if he asks for a fish, will instead of a fish give him a serpent? Or if he asks for an egg, will give him a scorpion? If you then, evil as you are, know how to give good gifts [gifts that are to their advantage] to your children, how much more will your heavenly Father give the Holy Spirit to those who ask and continue to ask Him!"
Luke 11:5-13 AMPC

"Ask, and it shall be given you; seek, and ye shall find; knock, and it shall be opened unto you: For every one that asketh receiveth; and he that seeketh findeth; and to him that knocketh it shall be opened. Or what man is there of you, whom if his son ask bread, will he give him a stone? Or if he ask a fish, will he give him a serpent? If ye then, being evil, know how to give good gifts unto your children, how much more shall your Father which is in heaven give good things to them that ask him?"
Matthew 7:7-11 KJV

What you ask GOD in Faith, HE will do:

"And Jesus answering saith unto them, Have faith in God. For verily I say unto you, That whosoever shall say unto this mountain, Be thou removed, and be thou cast into the sea; and shall not doubt in his heart, but shall believe that those things which he saith shall come to pass; he shall have whatsoever he saith. Therefore I say unto you, What things soever ye desire, when ye pray, believe that ye receive them, and ye shall have them. And when ye stand praying, forgive, if ye have ought against any: that your Father also which is in heaven may forgive you your trespasses. But if ye do not forgive, neither will your Father which is in heaven forgive your trespasses."
Mark 11:22-26 KJV

"And Jesus, replying, said to them, Have faith in God [constantly]. Truly I tell you, whoever says to this mountain, Be lifted up and thrown into the sea! and does not doubt at all in his heart but believes that what he says will take place, it will be done for him. For this reason I am telling you, whatever you ask for in prayer, believe (trust and be confident) that it is granted to you, and you will

[get it]. And whenever you stand praying, if you have anything against anyone, forgive him and let it drop (leave it, let it go), in order that your Father Who is in heaven may also forgive you your [own] failings and shortcomings and let them drop. But if you do not forgive, neither will your Father in heaven forgive your failings and shortcomings."
Mark 11:22-26 AMPC

When I ask According to HIS will, HE hears me and I receive it:

"And this is the confidence that we have in him, that, if we ask any thing according to his will, he heareth us: And if we know that he hear us, whatsoever we ask, we know that we have the petitions that we desired of him."
1 John 5:14-15 KJV

"And this is the confidence (the assurance, the privilege of boldness) which we have in Him: [we are sure] that if we ask anything (make any request) according to His will (in agreement with His own plan), He listens to and hears us. And if (since) we [positively] know that He listens to us in whatever we ask, we also know [with settled and absolute knowledge] that we have [granted us as our present possessions] the requests made of Him."
1 John 5:14-15 AMPC

I Want as Peaceful a Life as Possible:

"I exhort therefore, that, first of all, supplications, prayers, intercessions, and giving of thanks, be made for all men; For kings, and for all that are in authority; that we may lead a quiet and peaceable life in all godliness and honesty. For this is good and acceptable in the sight of God our Saviour; Who will have all men to be saved, and to come unto the knowledge of the truth. For there is one God, and one mediator between God and men, the man Christ Jesus; Who gave himself a ransom for all, to be testified in due time. Whereunto I am ordained a preacher, and an apostle, (I speak the truth in Christ, and lie not;) a teacher of the Gentiles in faith and verity. I will therefore that men pray every

where, lifting up holy hands, without wrath and doubting."
1 Timothy 2:1-8 KJV

"Most of all, I'm writing to encourage you to pray with gratitude to God. Pray for all men with all forms of prayers and requests as you intercede with intense passion. And pray for every political leader and representative, so that we would be able to live tranquil, undisturbed lives, as we worship the awe-inspiring God with pure hearts. It is pleasing to our Savior-God to pray for them . He longs for everyone to embrace his life and return to the full knowledge of the truth. For God is one, and there is one Mediator between God and the sons of men—the true man, Jesus, the Anointed One. He gave himself as ransom-payment for everyone. Now is the proper time for God to give the world this witness. I have been divinely called as an apostle to preach this revelation, which is the truth. God has called me to be a trustworthy teacher to the nations. Therefore, I encourage the men to pray on every occasion with hands lifted to God in worship with clean hearts, free from frustration or strife."
1 Timothy 2:1-8 TPT

CLOSING THOUGHTS

As I said from the beginning, this book is not deigned to be a prayer manual. It is the story of the impact prayer has made in my life. As HOLY SPIRIT leads, I will write a follow up to this book which will deal with specific prayers. Until that time, my desire is that everyone who reads this book will be challenged to seek the face of GOD. I pray that we will all gain a renewed passion for HIS presence. That we will become so consumed by that presence, it will cause us to long for a habitation lifestyle and not just a visitation experience.

One significant habit of the life of JESUS was HIS prayer life. We often see in the gospels that JESUS would pull away from the disciples to spend time with The FATHER in prayer.

"And it came to pass in those days, that he went out into a mountain to pray, and continued all night in prayer to God."
Luke 6:12 KJV

"Now in those days it occurred that He went up into a mountain to pray, and spent the whole night in prayer to God."
Luke 6:12 AMPC

"At about that same time he climbed a mountain to pray. He was there all night in prayer before God… ."
Luke 6:12-16 MSG

Still there were other occasions when JESUS chose to go into solitary places and spend time with HIS Father GOD.

"And when he had sent the multitudes away, he went up into a mountain apart to pray: and when the evening was come, he was there alone."
Matthew 14:23 KJV

"After sending them home, he went up into the hills by himself to pray. Night fell while he was there alone."
Matthew 14:23 NLT

"And after He had dismissed the multitudes, He went up into the hills by Himself to pray. When it was evening, He was still there alone."
Matthew 14:23 AMPC

"As soon as the meal was finished, he insisted that the disciples get in the boat and go on ahead to the other side while he dismissed the people. With the crowd dispersed, he climbed the mountain so he could be by himself and pray. He stayed there alone, late into the night."
Matthew 14:22-23 MSG

JESUS was fully aware of HIS status as the Son of GOD. He was aware that HE was positioned to demonstrate the life and power of The FATHER in the earth. HE was also aware that HE was living a life purposely designed to fulfill the plan and will of GOD. JESUS lived to please HIS Father. JESUS was so committed to pleasing HIS Father, that HE would do nothing without communicating with The FATHER to be sure that HIS actions represented The FATHER in every way. JESUS did not want to do anything that HIS Father did not approve of.

"For I have not spoken of myself; but the Father which sent me, he gave me a commandment, what I should say, and what I should speak."

John 12:49 KJV

"I don't speak on my own authority. The Father who sent me has commanded me what to say and how to say it."
John 12:49 NLT

"This is because I have never spoken on My own authority or of My own accord or as self-appointed, but the Father Who sent Me has Himself given Me orders [concerning] what to say and what to tell." [Deut. 18:18, 19.]
John 12:49 AMPC

"The things I taught were not from myself. The Father who sent me told me what to say and what to teach."
John 12:49 NCV

"If anyone hears what I am saying and doesn't take it seriously, I don't reject him. I didn't come to reject the world; I came to save the world. But you need to know that whoever puts me off, refusing to take in what I'm saying, is willfully choosing rejection. The Word, the Word-made-flesh that I have spoken and that I am, that Word and no other is the last word. I'm not making any of this up on my own. The Father who sent me gave me orders, told me what to say and how to say it. And I know exactly what his command produces: real and eternal life. That's all I have to say. What the Father told me, I tell you."
John 12:47-50 MSG

Getting in line with the mind and the heart of GOD HIS Father was the greatest priority of JESUS. JESUS knew how easily the stresses and day to day activities of life could pile up in our life, and be used as a tool of our enemy to get us off track and out of the will of GOD. So JESUS found time to fellowship with HIS Father. That is the aim of this book. It is my sincere desire that every reader will make time in your daily life to spend time in intimate fellowship with THE FATHER. Make your life a point of unified connectivity with the will and the heart of GOD. Make a decision to purposely get involved with the plans of Heaven for the lives of men and women in the earth. Allow HOLY SPIRIT to utilize your tongue. Speak, confess, and declare the word of GOD in your prayer life. Overwhelm and bring disruption and destruction to the enemy's plans and schemes, giving glory to our GOD. Make seeing the universal will of GOD for all mankind, as well as the personal will of GOD for your life come to pass, your highest priority.

"The Lord is not slack concerning his promise, as some men count slackness; but is longsuffering to us-ward, not willing that any should perish, but that all should come to repentance."
2 Peter 3:9 KJV

"The Lord does not delay and is not tardy or slow about what He promises, according to some people's conception of slowness, but He is long-suffering (extraordinarily patient) toward you, not desiring that any should perish, but that all should turn to repentance."
2 Peter 3:9 AMPC

"Don't overlook the obvious here, friends. With God, one day is as good as a thousand years, a thousand years as a day. God isn't late with his promise as some measure lateness. He is restraining himself on account of you, holding back the End because he doesn't want anyone lost. He's giving everyone space and time to change."
2 Peter 3:8-9 MSG

Everything we do and everything that has been done for us is done to successfully complete the plan and will of GOD. HE wants all mankind to be with HIM for eternity. HE has given us the opportunity to be a significant part of the plan and process of salvation in the lives of the people here in the earth. GOD wants all people to know that HE loves them unwaveringly, and unconditionally. HE wants all leaders, government, family, business, media, educational, artistic and entertainment, and religious leaders to live in unified fellowship with HIM. To accomplish this plan, The Kingdom of Heaven requires the participation and involvement of those who are living in a personal intimate relationship with GOD. Not everyone will accept the challenge, and say yes to the call. Everyone who doesn't will make an excuse for why they don't pray. GOD will love them anyway. However, those of us who do will find ourselves caught up in an experience that is truly powerful and life changing. We will experience things and get to know GOD in ways that can only be revealed through a, "personal and purposeful, passionate pursuit of HIS presence."

There is so much more that I could say. There are so many more personal experiences that I could share. I am certain that when you choose to pursue a lifestyle of intimate fellowship with The FATHER, you will be changed in ways that cannot be adequately described, they must be experienced. This is what I live for. I Live to Pray! GOD'S great grace to you, in this lifelong journey of personal fellowship with HIM.

"The first thing I want you to do is pray. Pray every way you know how, for everyone you know. Pray especially for rulers and their governments to rule well so we can be quietly about our business of living simply, in humble contemplation. This is the way our Savior God wants us to live. He wants not only us but everyone saved, you know, everyone to get to know the truth we've learned: that there's one God and only one, and one Priest-Mediator between God and us—Jesus, who offered himself in exchange for everyone held

captive by sin, to set them all free. Eventually the news is going to get out. This and this only has been my appointed work: getting this news to those who have never heard of God, and explaining how it works by simple faith and plain truth. Since prayer is at the bottom of all this, what I want mostly is for men to pray—not shaking angry fists at enemies but raising holy hands to God…"
1 Timothy 2:1-10 MSG

In this moment My FATHER GOD, I'm so thankful for an opportunity to share with the world, truths which YOU have shared with me throughout my lifetime. I can boldly say that not only have YOU shared with me in my past moments, I live in the expectation and excited anticipation of so much more that YOU will continue to share with me throughout all of the remaining moments of my life.

Wherever this book goes and whoever is touched by it, let there be an eternal impartation of a hunger for YOUR presence. I ask that the fire of the desire for more of YOU continue to grow and get greater within me until the person of Walter E. Roberts is totally consumed by the Person of THE FATHER who gave HIS Only Holy Spirit birthed Son JESUS to be CRIST for the world. Let the person of Walter and every other Human being whose life is touched by this book either personally or through someone else who has read it, be a harvest reaper and a world changer; until we have fulfilled the commission which JESUS gave us through HIS Disciples over 2100 years ago in the HOLY BIBLE book of St. Matthew 28. 18-20; and St. Mark 16.15,16 to go into the whole earth and share the gospel with every creature with full expectation of seeing people's hearts touched and minds changed as they are converted. Empower us to teach them to become disciples, in order to bring about the implementation of YOUR plan in the earth and YOUR will for Mankind.   IN JESUS' NAME I pray……………… AMEN, AMEN, AMEN!!!

I pray that we will be the manifestation of a generation of Davidic Worshipful Believers. David, after beginning to reign as King in Jerusalem over a finally unified nation, sought out the symbol of GOD'S presence and pursued it. David, when he could have lived comfortably on the throne as GOD'S chosen King, pursued The Ark of The Covenant as the physical representation of the presence of JEHOVAH and found it at the home of Obed Edom.

Saul had been King for 40 years. The Ark had been under the Philistines control for 20 years before Saul became King, and in his entire time as King in Jerusalem, he was comfortable without it. That's the way that many believers are today. They are comfortable just knowing that GOD is out there. But they have never personally pursued HIS Presence.

Which character will manifest in your life? Will you willingly live content knowing that GOD is alive, but trusting your pastor or "prayer warriors," to keep you covered? Or will you go after a personal relationship with THE FATHER, knowing that HE is alive and desires to participate in an intimate personal relationship with you. Then from the development of such a relationship, you won't have to depend on others to tell you what GOD wants for your life. You will be able to receive the insight which HOLY SPIRIT sends through others as a confirmation that you are in agreement with HIM , while you grow and become one who can disciple others for CHRIST.

Personal and Purposeful Passionate Pursuit of HIS Presence

Your Tongue Speaking the word of GOD in faith is the most powerful force in the earth.

  A. Prayer is not an accidental activity; it must be intentional.

You can pray, no matter what your current condition, or whether anyone else knows. You don't have to be seen to be relevant.

Scriptural References were taken from the following translations and versions of the HOLY BIBLE:

KJV- King James Version

AMPC- Amplified Bible, Classic Edition

NLT- New Living Translation

CEV- Contemporary English Version

NCV- The New Century Version

MSG- The Message

TPT- The Passion Translation

CEB- Common English Bible

DARBY- Darby's Translation 1890

Douay-Rheims Challoner Revision 1752

Easy English Bible 2018

GNTD- Good News Translation (US Version)

GW- GOD'S WORD Translation

GWC- St Paul from the TRENCHES 1916

Hebrew Names Version

HCSB- Holman Christian Standard Bible

JUB- Jubilee Bible

MEV- Modern English Version

NET- New English Translation

NMV- New Messianic Version

OJB- Orthodox Jewish Bible

TLV- Tree of Life Version

TS2009- The Scriptures 2009

WBMS- Wycliffe's Bible with Modern Spelling

WEB- World English Bible

WMB- World Messianic Bible

Young's Literal Translation 3ʳᵈ Revision 1898

Contact Information:

Apostle Walter E. Roberts
Presiding Bishop and Chief Apostle
HEAL THE NATIONS Global Fellowship of Ministries
PO Box 614
Tiffin, Iowa 52340
phone (319) 621-2486
email: treeforhealing@gmail.com

www.ingramcontent.com/pod-product-compliance
Lightning Source LLC
Chambersburg PA
CBHW050905160426
43194CB00011B/2295